LOST
FORT ELLIS

LOST FORT ELLIS

A FRONTIER HISTORY OF BOZEMAN

THOMAS C. RUST, PHD

FOREWORD BY DR. HARRY W. FRITZ

THE History PRESS

Published by The History Press
Charleston, SC 29403
www.historypress.net

Top front cover: *The Lookout* by Frederic Remington (1887).

First published 2015

Manufactured in the United States

ISBN 978.1.62619.979.8

Library of Congress Control Number: 2015933530

For Mom and Dad, whose unwavering support during my research made this possible. And to Aimee, Bridger, Jackson and Madison, whose patience allowed it to be published. And to Bill Walker, former history teacher at Bozeman Senior High School, who showed me that teaching history could be so fun.

CONTENTS

FOREWORD

We have numerous histories of military forts in the American West. We have local studies of the origins of Montana's cities and towns. But until now, no historian has put the two together. Thomas Rust fills a sizable gap in Montana historiography with this detailed account of the many interconnections between two early communities, separated by just three miles. Bozeman and nearby Fort Ellis enjoyed a symbiotic relationship. Neither, it seems, could have existed without the other. The fort allowed the city to grow and prosper until it could stand alone. Without Fort Ellis (1867–86), would Bozeman have survived?

Readers interested in the role Fort Ellis played in the Sioux and Nez Perce Wars or in the exploration of Yellowstone Park will be disappointed. They "will only smell the faintest whiff of gunpowder." But they will learn that the fort played an even more important role in securing the foundations of Montana. It allowed a frontier, nearly all-male "cumulative community" to become a stable, well-ordered, productive society.

In 1867, John Bozeman wrote to Acting Governor Thomas Francis Meagher and warned of the "imminent danger of hostile Indians." Meagher asked General William T. Sherman to authorize a federal militia. Meagher and Sherman disliked each other—the former was a "stampeder" and the latter a "rude and inconsiderate martinet." Both Bozeman and Meagher would die unnatural deaths in 1867, though not from Indian attacks. Indeed, the struggling city of Bozeman never faced a real Indian threat. Its difficulties stemmed from a lack of travelers after the army closed the Bozeman Trail and a lack of markets for the agricultural produce of the fertile East Gallatin

Valley. Fort Ellis, established on August 27, 1867, remedied all problems. It guarded the passes against perceived threats from the east, poured money into the local economy and purchased food and supplies from area farmers and merchants. It rescued Bozeman from possible disintegration.

As for Native Americans, soldiers at the fort never quite satisfied the hostile demands of citizens in the city. The army oscillated between demands for "utter extinction" and professions of "love for their conversion to civilization and Christianity." Locals favored the former while many officers promoted more benevolent attitudes, especially toward the nearby friendly Crows (Custer's scouts).

Soldiers spent their paychecks in town, and merchants competed for their money. Not surprisingly, alcohol caused the greatest tensions. The fort's commanders often sought to prohibit the sale and consumption of hard spirits, but such commerce thrived. Drunken soldiers often rioted, to the town's acute displeasure.

Such operational and economic activities characterized most military posts in the West. But they are not the thematic heart of this fine study. Tom Rust focuses on social and cultural interactions between fort and town, between soldiers and civilians. Fort Ellis introduced ethnic and social diversity to the Gallatin Valley. The sometimes uneasy interplay of nationalities, religions, educational levels, reform impulses (especially temperance) and the shifting sex ratio prompted both connections and conflict. Officers, mainly, and some married men mixed comfortably with the town's elite and middle classes at dances and theatrical productions. Common soldiers sought bars and prostitutes. Differences became exaggerated—the numbers of (male) soldiers declined over time as Bozeman grew more socially and economically diverse.

By the 1880s, with the Indian menace disappearing and the arrival of the Northern Pacific Railroad (1883), townspeople looked greedily upon the fort's thirty-two thousand acres of prime agricultural land. Fort Ellis's main contribution to Montana—the stabilization of Bozeman—had been accomplished. Thanks to Tom Rust, we now know how that happened.

HARRY W. FRITZ
Department of History
The University of Montana

ACKNOWLEDGEMENTS

This work originated with my master's thesis at the University of Denver. As such, many professors there had a profound influence on the final work. In particular, John Livingston and John Marshall were extremely helpful in reading drafts and challenging me to constantly improve the work. Of course, any errors are solely my own and no one else's.

INTRODUCTION

In 1873, the fledging city of Bozeman needed help. In true vigilante style, a riotous and drunken mob destroyed the log jail and took the inhabitants—a white drifter and an African American with connections to several of the city's brothels—and hanged them. The town's judge sent a message to nearby Fort Ellis's commanding officer, Colonel Hancock, requesting military aid to prevent the spread of the violence. Hancock personally led a detachment of the Second U.S. Cavalry to restore order. The irony of the soldiers' establishing order within the town must have been obvious to at least some of the longtime residents who remembered a date, some six years before, when soldiers purposefully came to town under orders to destroy one building and ransack two others. These two incidents exemplify the ambivalent relationship the army had with settlers on Montana's military frontier.

Bozeman and Fort Ellis provide a valuable opportunity to examine the complex interactions between civilian and military society. The complexity of their relationship created cooperation and conflict, dependence and the desire for autonomy, as well as support and indignation. While both societies had their own perspectives, aspirations and modes of conduct, their presence on the Montana frontier worked synergistically, even through their conflict, to develop the region economically and socially.

In recent years, military historians have begun to move beyond the examination of the study of troop movements and the focus on battles. For most soldiers, battle was a very limited element of their martial experience. The vast majority of their time in service was relegated to other much more mundane duties. While lacking the drama of combat, which is all too easily romanticized or glorified, the history written by the post–World War II generation has looked instead at the interaction of the military with and within society, in terms of economics, politics and culture. This study falls squarely in that category. Little attention is paid to the actual conflicts by Fort Ellis's troops with the tribes of the West. Readers will smell only the faintest whiff of gunpowder. Rather, it is hoped they will smell the liquor on the soldier's breath and hear the crack of the baseball bat, the music of the military ball or even the sounds of a saloon fight between a soldier and a civilian. This is not a story about pacifying the West by defeating the Indians. Rather, it is about the role of the military in the development and maintenance of civilian society in the region.

In examining the people who settled on the frontier, historians have separated the soldiers and civilians into distinct societies, which they were. However, they were societies that had frequent contact and interaction with each other. The investigation of the two societies' interaction has long been very limited. Those studies that did examine the army's interaction with the civilians focused primarily on the economic aspect. Robert Frazier's *Forts and Supplies: The Role of the Army in Building New Mexico* detailed the economic impact of the army in New Mexico before the Civil War, with an emphasis on the supplies required to maintain the posts in the Southwest. Frank N. Schubert's "Troopers, Taverns, and Taxes: Fort Robinson, Nebraska, and Its Municipal Parasite, 1886–1911," in Gary Ryan and Timothy Nenninger's *Soldiers and Civilians: The U.S. Army and the American People*, examined the role of the military payroll in a local community. Neither study examined the social relations initiated by the economic ties. Robert Wooster's narrative of Texas military life, *Soldiers, Sutlers, and Settlers: Garrison Life on the Texas Frontier*, came closest to examining in greater detail the civilian/soldier relationship. Still, Wooster continued to look at the relationship only through the eyes of the soldiers, examining civilians as they entered the daily mundane routine of the troopers. This study also lacked a general analysis.

Investigating the relationships and interaction between the soldiers and civilians on the frontier fills a void in historical study. They were distinct societies with their own rules of interaction. Each society had its own reason for being on the frontier. Yet through their mutual dependence, they interacted with each other and formed relations that included economic, civic and personal bonds that developed society and promoted social and economic stability as the region developed.

The communities of Bozeman and Fort Ellis, Montana, provide a convenient local study of the interaction between soldiers and civilians in the American West. As an isolated study, Bozeman and Fort Ellis provide suitable subject matter, but for a greater analysis of the significance of soldier-civilian interaction, the study of other forts and communities would be necessary in order to provide a means of comparison.

Fort Ellis was located in the agriculturally fertile Gallatin Valley to patrol the three passes through the mountains into the area. The town of Bozeman, three miles to the west of the fort, was a small village of fewer than one hundred people when the fort was established. With unsure economic prospects, the settlement had an uncertain future at best. Fort Ellis provided economic security by purchasing large quantities of supplies and by distributing the soldiers' paychecks through the local economy. As the town achieved economic stability, it began to develop from a settlement of rootless men into a community with developed families.

The fort and town shared a desire to combat many of the social problems that faced nineteenth-century society. Organizations that propagated middle-class Protestant values, compounded by the social hierarchy in military society, directly affected the relations between the populations of the town and fort. With the lack of women on the frontier, soldiers who ascribed to middle-class values enjoyed greater chances for interaction between the sexes.

The relationship between the different societies grew and developed as the conditions on the frontier changed. When the town had achieved more stability than in its early years, the relationship with the fort began to outlive its usefulness. In 1886, the town officially petitioned the War Department for the fort's abandonment.

Historians have frequently focused on the benefits that military posts had in the development of towns and regions. Historians Merrill G. Burlingame and Francis P. Prucha were among the first to study the role of the military in the West from a broad social and economic perspective and to examine its positive role in nation building. The economic studies of the military in the West continued to look at the favorable economic influence of the army in towns and regions. Robert Frazier, studying the antebellum Southwest, and Darlis Miller, studying the postwar Southwest, concluded that the U.S. Army was the largest economic force in the region and had provided a critical economic stimulus. Robert Wooster agreed and emphasized that the economic influence of a fort, which could "make or break local businessmen," proved essential to Texas's economic well-being in the frontier era. Most recently, Thomas T. Smith claimed that in the Texas frontier economy, the positive economic influence of the army went far beyond garrison towns. State politicians allied themselves with the War Department to benefit from a "military commercial" cooperative.

On a smaller scale, Darlis Miller suggested that each post in the Southwest deserved its own history "documenting its interaction with nearby settlers and its contribution to development." Such micro-studies likewise emphasize the positive economic aspects of the military on local communities. For example, Garna L. Christian's study of Fort Bliss and El Paso concluded that the fort's tremendous economic impact made El Paso dependent on the garrison. Robert Wooster's history of Fort Davis contended that military spending encouraged extensive nonmilitary development and that civilians remained largely dependent on that money. Thomas T. Smith's study of Fort Inge argued that military money had an inflationary impact on goods, real-estate values and services (including a 250 percent increase in local wages) during the history of the fort. While the positive influence of military money into a frontier economy was significant and should not be underemphasized, it is only part of the story. The civilian competition for that money brought tension and conflict, something studies to date have largely neglected. Only Garna Christian's study of Fort Bliss and El Paso hinted at that tension when Company A of the Twenty-fifth Infantry, an African American regiment, arrived at Fort Bliss. Christian claimed that with the regiment's arrival, the settlers "tallied the social and emotional expense of the base against the monetary and security rewards." In the end, Christian emphasized the importance of the fort's money on the fledgling town. While this approach is valid, it is nevertheless incomplete.

Fort Ellis and Bozeman, Montana, provide an example of how tensions and conflict arose in an often-tempestuous relationship of civilian and military economic interdependence. For the community, this tension was both internal (that is, between civilians in competition for economic resources the fort provided) and external (between the civilians and the military). At times, civilians, consciously aware of the economic potential of the fort, perfidiously took advantage of the post's dollars, adding to tension between the town and the fort. In a type of frontier mercantilism, Bozeman's businessmen acted both honestly and dishonestly to draw hard currency from the federal government into the local economy. Nevertheless, the economic input caused agitation in addition to needed economic stimuli.

Unlike many of the other towns of Montana in the 1860s, Bozeman was not a mining settlement. Settlers in the town schemed to take advantage of settlers traveling over the Bozeman Trail, a shortcut off the Oregon Trail. Located in the Gallatin Valley with its fertile volcanic soil, Bozeman would also be able to produce agricultural goods for the territory. Unforeseen by the early settlers was the government's problem with Native American raids along the trail and the agricultural slump in the territory that would threaten the town.

1
EARLY BOZEMAN AND THE ESTABLISHMENT OF FORT ELLIS

We have reliable reports here that we are in imminent danger.

As an agricultural community, Bozeman was an atypical settlement in Montana for the 1860s. The gold strikes in Montana in 1862–63 brought a wave of miners to the valleys and creek bottoms of the mountains. Many soon found that the rumors of the amount of gold outreached the reality of the situation. Still, miners came, some wanting to escape the Civil War and others just in the hope of quick riches. In that flood of adventurers came John M. Bozeman. A veteran of the gold rushes, he had followed his father to California in the 1850s and sought his own fortune in the gold fields of Colorado. Dissatisfied there, he came to Montana in the original rush of 1862.[1] Finding mining difficult in Montana, he decided to capitalize on the rush itself by providing his services as a trail guide.

There were three main route choices prior to 1863. The first, known as the Northern Overland Route, was very expensive, time consuming and characterized by searing heat in summer and bitter winds in winter. It also crossed through the highly contested lands of various tribes. This route started in Minnesota and crossed the northern Dakota Territory to the Missouri River, up the river to Fort Benton and then overland to Virginia City, Bannock or Helena. The second trail, the Corrine Route, was an out-of-the-way route off the Oregon Trail. From the east, settlers would leave from Missouri, proceed along the well-traveled Oregon Trail to Corrine, Utah, and then move north to Virginia City. The main disadvantage of this

John Bozeman, founder of the Bozeman Trail. *From* The Bozeman Trail, *vol. 2 (1922).*

route, other than going far out of the way, was the lack of fresh water. Nonetheless, it remained a popular route as it crossed territory less contested by tribes after the Fort Laramie Treaty of 1855. Father Pierre-Jean de Smet noted that traffic was so heavy that "not a blade of grass can shoot up" on it. The third route came from the west. Known as the Mullan Road, it reached from settlements in eastern Washington through the Deer Lodge Valley.

In 1863, Bozeman convinced his friend John Jacobs to head east with him and help establish a shortcut off the Oregon Trail. As the two started toward the Yellowstone River, they passed through the Gallatin Valley. The rich, black soil of the valley impressed John Bozeman with its agricultural potential. A year before, a small group of miners had left the gold fields near Virginia City and settled in the valley near the headwaters of the Missouri. The agricultural potential of the valley did not elude other people either. Mormon John Lyle Campbell wrote Brigham Young suggesting that a colony could be established with great ease. However, Young felt that the nearby mining boom culture would be incompatible with their religious values.[2]

Bozeman and his partner John Jacobs established their new trail, which cut northwest from the Oregon Trail at Independence Rock, passed through the hunting grounds of the Sioux and Northern Cheyenne Indians east of the Big Horn Mountains, up to the Yellowstone River and then turned west across the Rocky Mountains to Virginia City.

Bozeman and Jacobs made their first attempt to bring settlers over the trail in 1863, but the not-so-intrepid settlers turned back after only a few days when they learned that there was no military protection along the trail. The following year, they had more success when they successfully brought 40

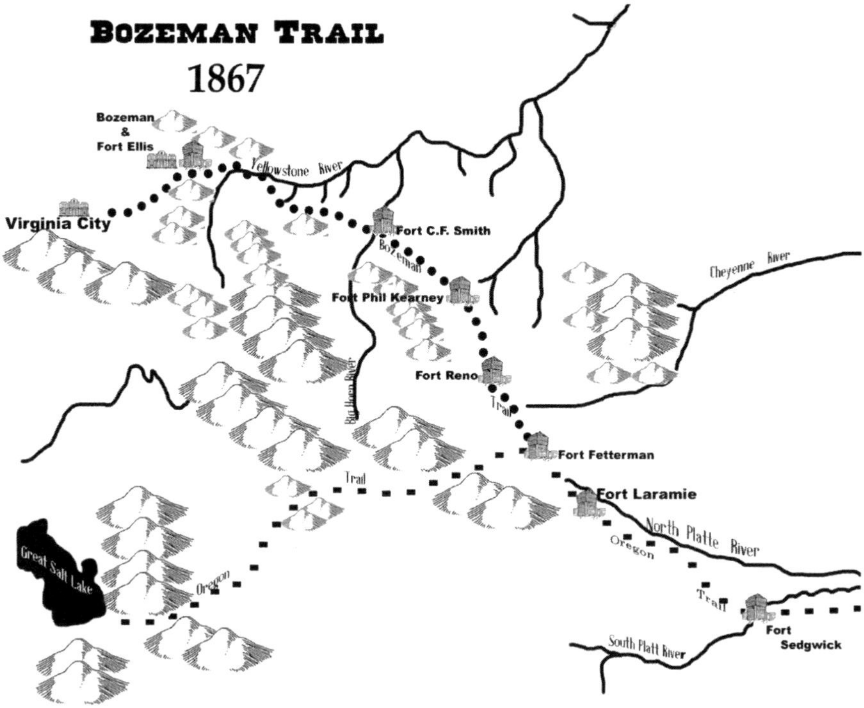

Bozeman Trail, 1867. *By author.*

wagons up the trail to Bozeman. Only a few days later, Jim Bridger arrived with another 125 wagons.[3] John Bozeman said he intended to return the next spring leading more migrants over his new route. He solicited the aid of William J. Beall and Daniel E. Rouse to organize and initiate a scheme of town speculation in the fertile Gallatin Valley.[4] A town could bring the men profits in two ways. First, the road-weary migrants would be greeted upon their descent from the mountains by a small urban center that could ease their suffering and provide much-needed supplies. Second, the town would grow as discouraged miners decided to give up searching for gold and silver and try farming instead. Settlers moving over the road also might be enticed to bypass mining altogether and begin farming immediately after their arrival from the east. The new town, soon named Bozeman City (or just Bozeman), was "standing right at the gate of the mountains" and was ready to "swallow-up all the tenderfeet that would reach the territory from the east, with golden fleeces to be taken care of."[5]

Virginia City, Montana, 1866. *Courtesy of the Library of Congress.*

As predicted, many migrants came over the trail looking for their golden dream. Albert J. Dickson followed his family over the Bozeman Trail to Virginia City in 1864 and confronted the question that faced many miners and families: "Where do we go from here?"[6] Virginia City was full of miners. Dickson claimed that "every foot of ground along the creek had been staked out," and there was no profitable place left to mine.[7] His family decided to try farming and left Virginia City for the new agricultural settlement of Bozeman. Dickson wrote that "it struck me rather oddly to be following in reverse order the very trail that we had vainly hoped to have a part in blazing."[8] The family stopped on the banks of the West Gallatin River, seven miles from Bozeman, and claimed land for farming.

The growth of agriculture in the valley around Bozeman flourished in the early years. Large quantities of staples such as wheat and barley, combined with abundant vegetable crops, produced enough food to feed the mining settlements of the territory. Within two years of the town's creation, citizens established two flour mills. In fact, the valley and other agricultural settlements in the territory produced too much food, and prices dropped as production increased.[9]

In addition to the economic insecurity, the fear of Indians also created anxiety for the early settlers. Travel over the Bozeman Trail had agitated local tribes of Sioux and Cheyenne and brought attacks on the settlers' wagon trains. In response, the army built a series of forts along the trail in Wyoming, but hostile activities continued.[10] The town of Bozeman, located between the territories of several tribes, was host to annual migrations across the valley by Plateau tribes from the west on their way to the hunting grounds in the Yellowstone Valley.[11] The settlers' loose stock and horses provided seductive objects for theft among the Indians. Consequently, despite the Indians' relatively harmless intentions toward the personal safety of the settlers, the Euro-American homesteaders, with their lack of understanding, dreaded the tribes.

The popularity of the Bozeman Trail, however, had become rather problematic for the army. As traffic increased over the trail, the Sioux and Northern Cheyenne attacked several trains. A series of treaties were signed with tribes in 1865 that proved to be an abysmal failure. The treaties stated that existing or established trails would be free from attack. However, the tribal representatives who signed the treaties did not fully represent the tribes. Some in the army were keenly aware of this. Major General John Pope wrote to his superiors that he did not consider the treaties "worth the paper they are written on" in the summer of 1866. He went on to add, "I have myself no doubt that hostilities will again break out."[12] New peace commissions were sent out to shore up the treaties in 1866. But again, only a few small tribes signed, and they did not represent the whole.

Yet not all in the army shared Pope's concern. E.B. White, the superintendent of Indian Affairs, claimed that the latest round of treaties was a success and that a "most cordial feeling prevails."[13] Newspapers echoed the sentiments, and even Lieutenant General Sherman, commanding the Division of the Missouri, made only a halfhearted effort to fortify the trail in 1866 by sending out too few men who were ill equipped. He even encouraged the officers to take their families.[14] By December, after months of open hostility, it became poignantly clear that the army's efforts were insufficient when Captain William Fetterman and eighty-one of his men were killed in battle not far from Fort Phil Kearny, Wyoming, along the trail. Investigations followed, but John Sandborn of the Interior Department laid the blame squarely at the foot of the army. "The difficulty 'in a nutshell' was that the commanding officer of the district [Colonel Henry B. Carrington] was furnished no more troops or supplies for this state of war than had been provided and furnished him for a state of profound peace."[15]

Whatever the politicians thought in Washington mattered little to the people in the Gallatin Valley. In the spring of 1867, the citizens of Bozeman felt extremely uneasy about their situation. Several small raids on stock

The Fetterman Fight as depicted in *Harper's Weekly*, March 23, 1867.

inflated the sense of danger, and fear seemed very real that the war along the Bozeman Trail would reach Bozeman. In April 1867, William Alderson wrote that there was "quite an Indian scare at Bozeman and [the] Valley" on account of recent raids, in response to which the citizens proposed "to erect a stockade at Bozeman City."[16] There was some division about building the stockade during the next week, but the situation seemed desperate enough that John Bozeman wrote to the acting governor, Thomas Meagher, for assistance:

> *General:*
> *I take the responsibility of writing you a few lines for the benefit of the people of Montana. We have reliable reports here that we are in imminent danger of hostile Indians, and if there is not something done to protect this valley soon, there will be but a few men and no families left in Gallatin Valley. Men, women, and children are making preparations to leave at an early day. If you can make arrangements to protect them, they will stay. If not, this valley will doubtless be evacuated.*[17]

The governor sought permission from the War Department to raise a militia. Lieutenant General William T. Sherman, in command of the Military

Department of the Missouri, refused several of these pleas since any force of armed civilians would operate on its own and only complicate the already difficult situation in the region.[18]

Thomas Frances Meagher during the Civil War when he was a brigadier general of the Sixty-ninth New York Militia, better known as the "Irish Brigade." Meagher was the acting governor of Montana from September 1865 to October 1866. *Courtesy of the Library of Congress.*

John Bozeman was killed near the Yellowstone River a month after he wrote Meagher. When word reached the town that Indians had reportedly murdered its namesake, a panic ran through the valley and the territory.[19] Meagher went over Sherman and even general of the army U.S. Grant's head to Secretary of War Stanton for permission to raise his militia. Stanton and Grant briefed the president and gave Sherman permission to authorize the mustering of a force if the situation merited it, keeping in mind the potentially "very serious evils besides the enormous expenditure" that such a force might incur.[20] Meagher besieged Sherman not to delay, but old animosities flared between the two former Civil War colleagues. Meagher had publicly called Sherman a "rude and envenomed martinet" in 1861, an insult Sherman would not easily forgive.[21] Though cautious, Sherman realized that the situation could very well be beyond what the army in Montana could handle at the time. However, he felt that that Meagher should not be given the sole authorization to raise such a militia since "civilians of the style of T. Francis Meagher may involve the frontier in a needless war."[22] Sherman even reprimanded Meagher for sending telegrams collect to him.[23]

Killing of Col. Bozeman and wounding of Thos. Cover by the Black-feet Indians!.

THE PANIC AMONG THE GALLATIN SETTLERS!

THEIR APPREHENSIONS OF A GENERAL ATTACK UPON THEIR HOMES.

Their Appeal to Governor Meagher and the People of the Territory!

Prompt and friendly response by the Governor, and Minute Men called for to meet the emergency!

THE PEOPLE OF MADISON COUNTY RALLYING!

300 Men from Edgerton, and 100 from Deer Lodge Wanted!

LET THESE COUNTIES DO THEIR WHOLE DUTY!

Newspaper headline announcing the death of John Bozeman. *From the* Helena Weekly Herald, *May 2, 1867.*

Sherman also quietly sent Major William H. Lewis to Montana to independently investigate the situation and help organize the militia if needed. Lewis recommended a force of eight hundred men be raised for two months.[24] Reluctantly, General Sherman agreed to pay, arm and feed the militia at the expense of the government. Meagher, a former brigadier general of the famed Irish Brigade during the Civil War, appointed himself commander. However, Sherman's doubts about the situation appear to have been justified as no conflicts took place.

When Brigadier General Alfred H. Terry, commander of the Department of Dakota, arrived to inspect the situation later in the summer, he was of the "opinion that [the] troops should be mustered out."[25] He went on to claim that a "great alarm was honestly felt by the people of [the Gallatin] Valley" but that "nothing which had happened within the Territory…justified the

Brigadier General Alfred Terry from the Brady-Handy Collection of the Library of Congress. Terry had a celebrated Civil War career before coming west in the postbellum years. He was a key figure in the negotiation of the Fort Laramie Treaty (1868) before returning to the East to take over the Third Military District of the South during Reconstruction. He returned to the West during the Sioux War of 1876–77 and the Nez Perce War of 1877. In 1886, he was promoted to command of the Military Division of the Missouri. *Courtesy of the Library of Congress.*

alarm which was felt." However, he nonetheless authorized the creation of a post in the area anyway.[26]

Although the nice little war that Meagher envisioned never developed, the Bozeman merchants lined their pockets with government money. During the militia's "Montana Picnic," Captain E.W. Clift of the regular army arrived to identify potential locations for a permanent military post in the valley.[27] By the fall of that year, Captain Robert S. LaMotte arrived with two companies of the 13th United States Infantry and began construction of a military post to be named Fort Ellis after Colonel Augustus Van Horn Ellis of the 124th New York Volunteers, who had fallen in the defense of Little Round Top at the Battle of Gettysburg.

On August 31, 1867, LaMotte wrote to his superiors at Fort Shaw:

> *I have the honor to report that...on examining the surrounding country, I have located and commenced building a Post...situated in the Gallatin Valley at the extreme eastern end, at the opening of Bozeman's Pass and about three miles from the town of Bozeman. Bridger's Pass is about three miles west or northwest, and Flathead Pass about fifteen miles northwest.*[28]

LaMotte's location provided easy control of two of the three passes into the valley, but when Lieutenant Colonel Samuel B. Holabird inspected the fort two years later, he noted, "It is the general judgment of any intelligent person that a better site for a post exists but a short distance from the present one, upon higher ground." He went on to note that the construction of the buildings was relatively poor and that the fort was enclosed with "an unnecessarily high stockade, excluding the air, and making the place seem more like a prison than a military post." He added that the stockade should be immediately torn down. Yet the post was in most ways "sufficient for its need."[29]

Monument honoring August Van Horne Ellis (depicted in the statue atop), colonel (brevet brigadier general) of the 124th New York Volunteer Infantry, known as the "Orange Blossoms." Ellis was shot through the head near the Devil's Den at Gettysburg on July 2, 1863, where the monument now stands. *Author's collection.*

LaMotte also reported unfavorably on the Montana Militia's activities, which had not included any of the expected Indian encounters. He stated that the militia men were "as much dreaded by the people as the Indians, being a disorganized lawless

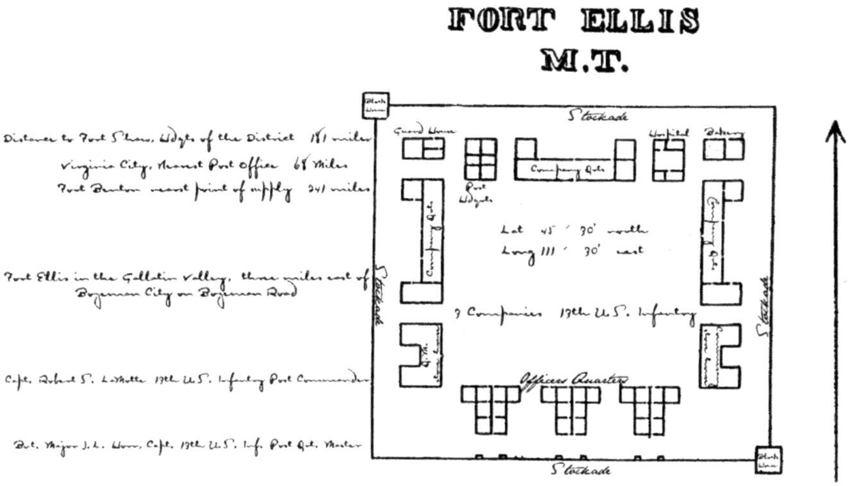

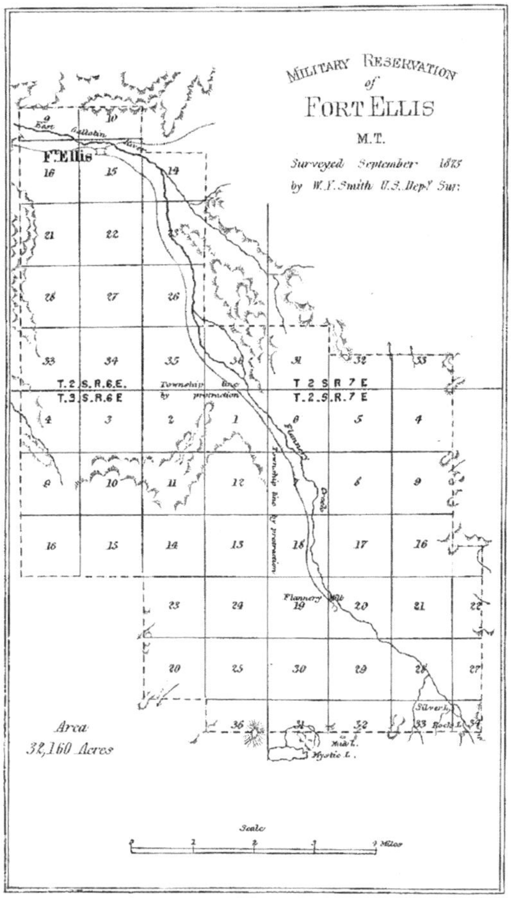

Above: Plan of Fort Ellis, 1868. The fort still has a stockade around the main buildings in this plan. Lieutenant Colonel Samuel Holabird described the stockade as "unnecessarily high" and made the fort "feel more like a prison than a military post." The stockade was removed shortly afterward. *Courtesy of Renne Library Special Collections, Montana State University, Bozeman, Montana. (Image modified for clarity and legibility.)*

Right: Map of Fort Ellis Military Reservation. *From* Outline Descriptions of the Posts in the Military Division of the Missouri *(1876)*.

set of desperados under no sort of discipline whatever." Their activities while they were "in service" were not amusing to LaMotte. "Out of five hundred sent there, only fifty remain, the rest either being on indefinite furlough, prospecting or riding public horses back and forth between Bozeman and their camps for whiskey." He went on to note that several of the government's horses "have been stolen lately in the vicinity and I see the Montana papers are filled with accounts of these 'Indian depredations.' I noticed, however, that in this vicinity, the depredators are strongly suspected of being the Montana Militia."[30] With the presence of regular troops at Fort Ellis and the nefarious behavior of the militia, the U.S. Army ordered that they be mustered out of service the following month, to which the territorial governor protested but complied.[31]

The continued hostilities along the Bozeman Trail throughout 1867, which became known as Red Cloud's War, forced the army to acknowledge the futility of defending it. Manpower, resources and money were being wasted defending a route that the Indians proved they could sustain their attacks on and effectively halt traffic. In addition, it was becoming clear that the transcontinental railroad would be completed in just a few years and that immigrant traffic could more easily, safely and economically come north from Utah along the Corrine Route.[32] By March 2, 1868, the general of the U.S. Army, Ulysses S. Grant, issued orders for posts along the route to be abandoned, and travel along the trail was forbidden.[33]

The draw of eastern migrants through Bozeman ceased, and the town could expect little money from immigrant travel in the next years. Townsman Peter Koch claimed that the abandonment of the trail "closed the front gate to Montana, and Fort Ellis became the gatekeeper."[34]

2
THE DIFFICULTIES OF COMMAND ON MONTANA'S MILITARY FRONTIER

My duties...are not so clearly laid down.

Major Nathaniel B. Sweitzer had a problem. As the commander of Fort Ellis, he found himself in a precarious situation in the summer of 1873. A group of settlers from nearby Bozeman had decided to venture down the Yellowstone Valley to the mouth of the Big Horn River to prospect for gold. However, Sweitzer saw potential danger. These adventurers were going into the heart of unseeded territory frequented by the hostile Sioux. They were also going near the more friendly Crow Reservation, which might also create problems. The settlers did not seem to have an accurate understanding of the complex tribal situation, seeing all Indians as a threat, and for years had claimed frequent attacks to stir the military to action to rid the area of Indians. This appeared to be a not-so-subtle effort to force the army into action.

Sweitzer and several of the other officers at the fort knew that not all tribes were hostile. He and even some of his most combat-minded predecessors discerned that the reports of native hostility were often exaggerated at the least or fabricated at the worst. In any case, Sweitzer surely must have known how thin the army was spread across Montana. These settlers could easily provoke hostilities that the army might not be fully prepared to deal with at that time. Yet, as the consummate professionals they were, the commanders of the fort followed orders, but there seemed a lack of consistency, even from the highest levels. Seeing the potential danger, not fully trusting the motives of the settlers, wanting to protect the army's Crow allies and without clear direction from above, Sweitzer telegraphed his superiors in St. Paul, requesting "information whether the Government would interfere to prevent such expedition and what action would be necessary in the case of Government interference."[35]

Fort Ellis provides a valuable case study into the difficulties of commanding a fort on Montana's military frontier. Military documents, letters and newspaper accounts reveal the frustration of U.S. Army officers regarding the difficult position in which they found themselves. Their dual mission of protecting civilians from Indian incursions but also Indians from settler's provocations and exploitation proved difficult given the army's tendency to succumb to political pressure brought by leading citizens of the nation and territory. The military commanders at posts like Fort Ellis had to diplomatically navigate Montana's military frontier, which consisted of complex relationships between the U.S. Army and its officers stationed in the territory, the civilian settlers, the territorial government and the native tribes that inhabited the region. The settlers and the army rarely agreed on either the nature or scope of the Indian "problem." Civilians often fabricated, exaggerated or provoked incidents with Indians to prod military action. They were also willing to exert political influence to achieve their ends of removing the Indians. The U.S. Army's unwillingness to take hasty action without reasonable cause and the lack of a clearly defined national policy led to tensions between soldiers and civilians. This tension existed not only within the territory but also at the highest policy-making levels, which resulted in unclear and inconsistent guidelines about the army's role in the West. Post commanders, perhaps most keenly aware of the actual condition in their given area, were left without an understanding of the army's desire of how to respond to rapidly changing situations. The frustrations felt by post commanders forced them to repeatedly seek clarification and voice their bewilderment, thus creating an inefficient response exacerbated by a dysfunctional communication loop with superiors far removed from local situations.

Fort Ellis was founded in the ad hoc military policy of the U.S. Army in 1860s Montana. Originally, a defensive perimeter of posts was to be constructed from Fort Benton in the north to protect the Missouri River route into Montana to Fort Shaw in the west to protect the mining settlements located there, and a new post on the upper Yellowstone River would be built to supplement Fort C.F. Smith on the Big Horn River to the south for the protection of the Bozeman Trail and to prepare the way for the Northern Pacific Railroad.[36] However, the situation changed rapidly in 1867 when the

A photo of Fort Ellis, Montana, looking south, taken in July 1871 by William Henry Jackson during the Hayden Survey of what would become Yellowstone National Park. *Courtesy of the National Park Service Archives.*

army decided to abandon the Bozeman Trail after Red Cloud's War and increased Indian activity near the infant settlement of Bozeman forced the government to abandon the defense of the Bozeman Trail.

If Generals Sherman or Terry thought that the presence of troops in the Gallatin Valley would assuage the fears of the settlers, they were sadly mistaken. The settlers continued to press for not only a greater number of troops but also frequent and direct military action. The valley was home to no tribe, but many had traditionally crossed it to and from hunting grounds on the Yellowstone River, even after pioneers founded their settlements. While tribes of Nez Perce, Flatheads and Bannocks typically did not have hostile intent, white response was predictably cautious and racist. In her diary, settler Sarah Tracy recollected that the "whole prairie south of town seemed covered with Indian tepees. Indian ponies, squaws, papooses, and dogs were everywhere." She claimed that they "would peer in the windows if the doors were locked, or come flocking around the door begging for biscuits, soap, clothes, everything."[37] The *Bozeman Avant Courier* claimed that when the Indians arrived, "their dusky forms…presented quite a grotesque appearance passing through the streets" and lamented that they thought the

In the Lodges of the Blackfeet Indians, by Frederic Remington, from *Harper's Weekly*, July 23, 1887. The Blackfeet were one of the tribes known to occasionally cross the Gallatin Valley, as were the Crow, the Sioux, the Shoshone, the Bannock and the Nez Perce.

tribes were "considerably on the increase."[38] While trading opportunities existed, the settlers had little sympathy for the natives peaceably traveling through the valley to their hunting grounds since they felt, as one later put it, that "the more Indians who starved to death the fewer we had to fight."[39] It was, they thought, the duty of the army to destroy the Indians. The editor of the *Avant Courier* frustratingly claimed, "The Army is only trying to keep the peace and is doing nothing to get rid of the Indian."[40]

Even with the presence of troops, settlers did not feel safe going far beyond town unless fully armed,[41] and the paper often sensationally reported rumors of "the slaughter of one or more of our race by the murderous redskins."[42] It editorialized that the number of soldiers was "always inadequate," even at times where no clear threat was imminent.[43] When troops were increased, the editors always wished for more. The *Courier* reported in 1871 that seventy-five infantry troops were en route to the fort but that "it should be better if the number were 1,000 mounted cavalry" since there was a "necessity for an increased number of troops to protect our frontiers…which have been the scene of annual raids from hostile savages that have been characterized by murder and robbery, since the first pioneers marked the wilderness with the progress of civilization."[44] They would raise concerns in the valley by reporting the departure of troops in the routine movements and were not above directly contacting officials in Washington about their concern, forcing the secretary of war to telegram the town and reassure them that "when troops move from Fort Ellis, it will be to operate against the Indians from whom the petitioners apprehend trouble."[45] Frustrated with what they saw as military inaction, it was not uncommon to use hyperbole to describe the danger and the possible ramifications. A small horse raid in 1871 was quickly settled by troops from Fort Ellis. However, the territorial governor painted the situation as desperate. He wrote to the secretary of the interior that the valley "is entirely unguarded and the citizens (and there are none better) are entirely at the mercy of the Indians, and many contemplate an early return to the East unless they can be protected." He went on to explain that "A stampede to the East…would be damaging to the future of the Great Northwest."[46] When the secretary of the interior forwarded the concerns to the secretary of war, the latter pragmatically responded, "It is not thought advisable to strengthen that particular section…at the expense of other points equally exposed."[47]

Commanders at the fort knew the reports to be often exaggerated or false. The reported raid in 1871 forced Major Eugene M. Baker to clarify the situation with Governor Potts. "The reports of an Indian raid last week in the Gallatin Valley are wholly false." He candidly stated, "It seems probable this is merely another effort to get troops by magnifying dangers, when they do exist, or by inventing them when short of the facts."[48] The lack of action by commanders frustrated the civilians to the extent that they considered taking matters into their own hands. During the winter of 1871–72, a movement to create an independent militia began. "Our citizens," the *Courier* reported, "despairing of adequate military protection, are going to throw themselves into the breech."[49] Since the editor felt that "one ounce of prevention is worth a pound of cure…preemptory measures must be adapted to secure general safety."[50] In 1873, the paper again encouraged citizens to be proactive in their defense. "It is not our desire to create unnecessary alarm, but we wish to enjoin on our citizens…the necessity of making preparations to resist Indian raids into our valley this summer."[51]

The commanders of Fort Ellis no doubt responded to such professional criticisms with ambivalence. Major Eugene Baker, a combat-minded Indian fighter who cannot be criticized for being soft on the Indians, felt the sting of such denunciations since they "usually placed the army in criticism of the entire Territory."[52] The relationship with local civilians was already

This photo of officers of Fort Ellis was taken in July 1871 by William Henry Jackson. Officers pictured (from left to right) are First Lieutenant Frank C. Grugan, Captain Lewis Thompson, Second Lieutenant George H. Wright, Second Lieutenant Gustavus C. Doane, Captain Lewis Cass Forsyth, Assistant Surgeon A.B. Campbell, Dr. R.M. Whitefoot, First Lieutenant Sam T. Hamilton, Major (Brevet Lieutenant Colonel) Eugene Baker (commanding post), Captain Edward Ball, Second Lieutenant Lovell H. Jerome, Captain George L. Tyler (front with arm on rail), Second Lieutenant Eward J. McClernand and Second Lieutenant Charles B. Scholfield. *Courtesy of the Library of Congress.*

complicated at best, and these disparagements only made things worse. While townsmen loved the infusion of the military payroll into the economy and social relations could often be warm, there was also a fairly significant amount of conflict.[53] While the military's primary mission was to protect the pioneers and open the West to settlement, the commanders were in a complicated position and left to navigate many competing demands. In addition, they shared not only a different perception of their mission but also a more nuanced view of the Indian situation than did the local civilian population.

Settlers were quick to sound the alarm at the sight of Indians, "hostile" or not, and when the army was called on to protect citizens in so many different places, fort commanders found themselves frustrated and often refused to help. For instance, Dr. A.J. Hunter created a health spa at a hot springs sixty miles from Bozeman in the Yellowstone River Valley not far from the Crow

Dr. Andrew Jackson Hunter's health spa, from Leeson's *History of Montana* (1885). The spa was located in the Yellowstone River Valley not far from the Crow Indian Reservation near present-day Big Timber, Montana, some sixty miles from Fort Ellis. Dr. Hunter built his spa at a hot springs frequented by Indians before white settlement in the area. The isolated location limited the protection the fort could offer from perceived "hostile" threats. Nonetheless, Dr. Hunter's daughter, Mary, ultimately married Lieutenant Gustavus Doane of the Second U.S. Cavalry stationed at Fort Ellis.

Indian Reservation. In 1874, he called on the fort for protection, but the commander, Major Nathaniel B. Sweitzer, responded:

> *The demand for troops is greater than can be supplied and none can be sent to guard such an isolated and unimportant point merely for the convenience of one party who has pushed his family beyond where any prudent man would locate them.*[54]

If the civilians usually referred to all natives in racist terms, the official and personal correspondence of the officers generally took pains to distinguish the difference between "hostile" tribes, such as the Sioux, and more friendly tribes, such as the Crow.[55] In fact, several officers held a general empathy for Indian culture.[56] This ambivalence toward Native Americans was not uncommon among many officers across the service,[57] and it is clear that

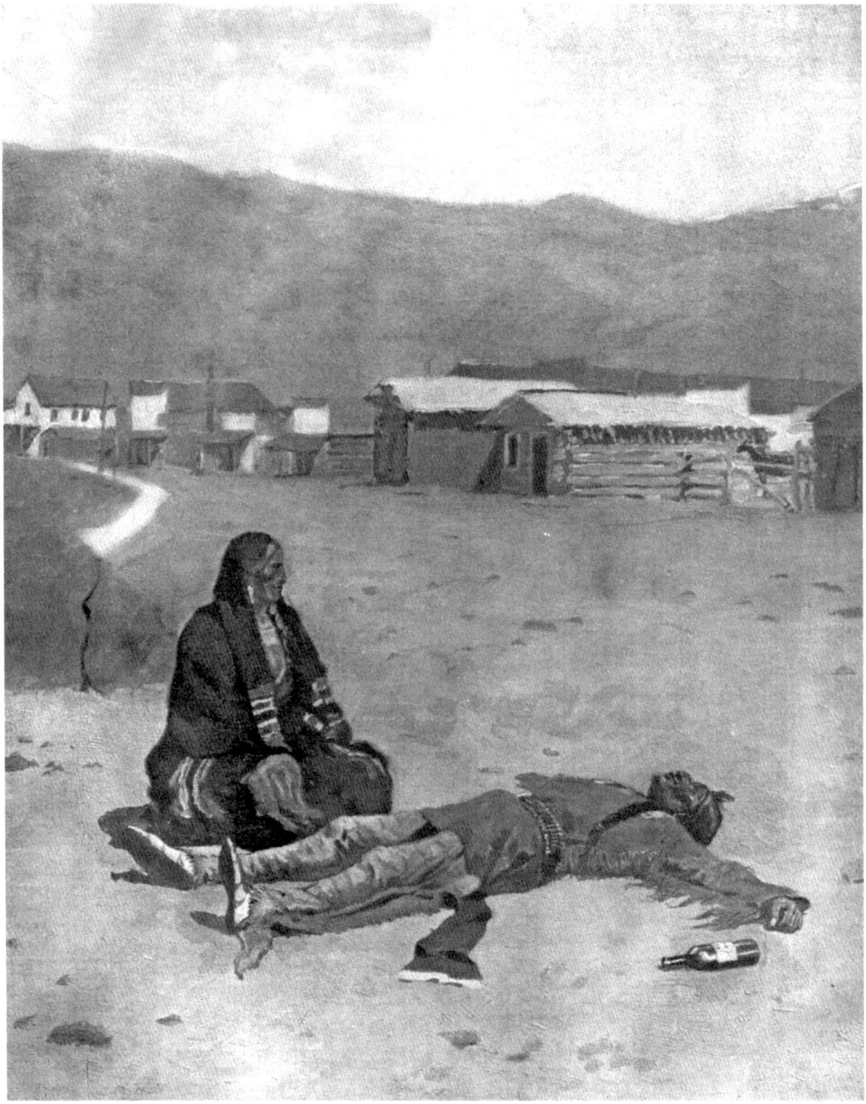

Red Man's Load. From Frederic Remington's Done in the Open *(1903).*

Fort Ellis had its share of Indian supporters. Major James S. Brisbin, one-time commander of Fort Ellis, wrote several essays for the *Chicago Tribune* in defense of the Indian—who, he claimed, had become "only what we have made him"—after he retired as a brigadier general.[58] He asserted, "Civilization brings its benefits and its pleasures but it brings also its duties and penalties and the verdict of important history." He claimed "during the last century we have done nothing for the Indian worth mentioning unless it has been to rob him of his land and cheat him out of his just dues and rights. Our Indian policy, as a great writer recently said, has been a 'century of dishonor.'"[59]

Several junior officers also held sympathetic views of Indians. Lieutenant James Bradley, stationed at Fort Shaw, wrote a lengthy poem entitled "The Early Races of America" that compared their unwritten history to the great civilizations of Egypt, Greece and Rome:

Ten thousand hands for years employed
And that the highest skill enjoyed
Must have united to upraise
What e'en in ruins does amaze.
Here palaces and temples rise
In polished stone of wondrous size
There lifts a massive pyramid
As grand as aught that Egypt did;
And road and rampart, tower and tomb,
Of age enwrapped in deepest gloom,
The work of nationals all unknown
If shown not in laconic stone.[60]

He went on to wonder what lessons of the Virgils, Demosthenes or Platos of their civilization have been lost to the detriment of mankind.

Had any record been preserved
Of all the varied deeds then done,
Now buried in Oblivion!
How might have seemed in contrast tame,
The classic tales of Greece and Rome,
And learned the youth of every land
Of sturdy virtue lessons grand
Instead of seeking in the pages
Of ancient Greek and Roman sages.
But none can pierce the gathered gloom,
Or raise the history from its tomb.
Time's curtain darkly thrown around.[61]

Unfortunately, two pages of the poem book are missing with the poem's end, but clearly Bradley had an admiration of Indian culture, which makes his death in 1877 at the Battle of the Big Hole only more ironic. His comparison of the Indian cultures to those of the great ancient societies of Western civilization is indicative of how soldiers ethnocentrically measured Native Americans rather than accepting them on their own terms.[62]

The role that Fort Ellis played in the administration of the nearby Crow Reservation appears to have influenced the development of these sympathetic sentiments toward Native Americans but also added to the frustrations of post commanders. A long-standing rivalry existed between the War Department and the Department of the Interior as to who could best administer the reservations. Few national politicians paid particular attention to the reservation problem. However, when President Grant took office, he made it a point to administer the reservations fairly and initially put their control under military officers whom he hoped would administer them in a forthright way under his "Peace Plan."[63] However, partisan political conflicts in Congress brought an end to the military administration when a bill passed forbidding army officers from serving as agents. This was partly in response to Fort Ellis's own Major Eugene Baker and his attack on the Piegan Indians in January 1870 that left 173 Indians, 53 of whom were women and children, dead on the frozen prairie of Montana, mobilizing national reformers who had influence in Congress.[64] Grant then proposed that churches choose the agents to run the agencies. The Methodist churches chose most of the agents in eastern Montana while the Catholic Church selected agents in the western part of the territory.

The army, however, continued to provide a supportive role on the reservations even if it was somewhat ill defined. The ambiguous demands of the Crow Agency further burdened the commanders. Not only were they called on to inspect supplies but also to prevent settlers from encroaching or attacking the reservation tribes. In 1874, a frustrated Sweitzer wrote to the assistant adjutant general of the department that "my duties in relation to the Indians and Agencies are not so clearly laid down."[65] Still exasperated a year later, he wrote directly to Lieutenant General Phillip Sheridan, commander of the Division of Missouri, lamenting his many unclear and potentially conflicting responsibilities:

> *I am continually called on for troops by agents to…cooperate with their Indians in their tribal wars…while we are held responsible for the protection of the settler, as well as bands of Bannocks, Nez Perce, and Flathead that are continually passing through settlements and who are liable to be attacked.*[66]

The military's role on the reservations only further frustrated the relationship between the fort and civilians. The assignments were vague and may have created inconsistencies in the way military officials handled agents' requests for action. When the contraband items like whiskey were confiscated, settlers might lash out in the pages of the *Courier*.[67] The animosity became perhaps most vitriolic when Captain Edward Ball accused Bozeman businessman Nelson Story not only of providing rancid pork to the reservation as part of his government contract with the agency but also of bribing Ball to approve the shipments. The accusations went before a grand jury, and while Story escaped indictment, the judge reprimanded the jury since the evidence seemed to favor such.[68]

Being in close contact with the friendly Crows and witnessing firsthand the dastardly treatment of them by the local settlers probably only further increased the commanders' sympathies for at least some Native Americans. Captain D.W. Benham of the Seventh U.S. Infantry was temporarily stationed at the agency to inspect arriving supplies and wrote back to Major Brisbin, commanding Fort Ellis, that "the Crow Indians have in every reasonable way shown themselves to be the fast friends of the white man, and in proportion to their advantages, loyal and true to the Government."[69]

Crow Indians Firing into the Agency by Frederic Remington. *From* Harper's Weekly, *November 5, 1887.*

He added, with a certain level of frustration, that in his "opinion the Crows have been misused...The Army has little to do with Indian matters but there are times when it is proper for any class of men to speak in defense of a wronged people and I believe such a time has come in the history of our dealings with the Crows."[70]

The frustration of these officers at Fort Ellis was found not only in their complicated relationship with the local civilians but also the vicissitudes felt due to national political vagaries regarding the desired size of a peacetime military, its compatibility with democratic institutions, and the complications with Reconstruction in the South.[71] The U.S. Army struggled to make a consistent Indian policy given the realities of partisan politics. The overall goal was the opening of the West for settlement, but the question of how to clear the region of its indigenous population became contentious. Congress, usually at the behest of motivated religious groups and private individuals, could influence the policy through army funding. The largest issue was where to place the Bureau of Indian Affairs, which frustrated military commanders. Its movement from the War Department to the Department of the Interior in 1849 at the behest of many reformers who saw the military's main mission as incompatible with civilizing the tribes seemed unsound to most military minds.[72] In 1867, general of the army U.S. Grant voiced his frustration to Secretary of War Stanton, claiming that "if the present practice is to be

Major General Philip H. Sheridan from the Brady-Handy Collection of the Library of Congress. Sheridan had a distinguished Civil War career before coming west in the immediate postbellum years. First, he was appointed to the Military District of the Southwest before appointment to the Fifth Military District in the Reconstruction-era South in 1866. In 1867, he assumed command of the Military Department of the Missouri. Ultimately, Sheridan would rise to the army's highest position, commanding general of the army, after William T. Sherman in 1883. *Courtesy of the Library of Congress.*

continued, I do not see that any course is left open to us, but to withdraw our troops to the settlements or call upon congress to provide the means and the troops to carry on formidable hostilities against the Indians until all Indians or all the whites…are exterminated."[73]

Congress, however, was at the mercy of vacillating public opinion. At times, reformers held great sway with a minority of politicians who could influence the debate about Indian policy in an otherwise indifferent Congress.[74] These reformers wished to help the Indians in the same way that the African Americans had been helped after the Civil War. Yet at other times, the reformers were more marginalized when other groups more hostile to the Indians periodically had influence.

The army would need to respond adequately to whichever had the most influence at the given time. Lieutenant General Phillip Sheridan, who has often wrongly been quoted as saying "the only good Indian is a dead Indian,"[75] had complained to General Sherman about the maddening influence of politics in the execution of his duties. Sherman responded that he should not "be unhappy about Indian affairs. There are two classes of people, one demanding the utter extinction of the Indians, and the other full of love for their conversion to civilization and Christianity. Unfortunately, the army stands between and gets the cuffs from both sides."[76] His affirmation did little to ease the fiery Sheridan's frustration, who wrote back with a rather insightful assessment of the ambivalent nature of the Indian-army relationship and the difficulties of public opinion:

> *The soldiers do not want to kill Indians. After long years of Indian frontier service, and I am satisfied that they are the only good practical friends that Indians have. We cannot avoid being abused by one side or the other. If we allow the defenseless people on the frontier to be scalped and ravished, we are burnt in effigy and execrated as soulless monsters, insensible to the sufferings of humanity. If the Indian is punished to give security to these people, we are the same soulless monsters from the other side. This is a bad predicament to be in; but as I have said, I have made my choice, and I am going to stand by the people the government has placed me here to protect.*[77]

Sherman's annoyance, however, was partially his own doing. When he assumed the position of general of the army in 1869, he purposely chose to keep the army out of partisan politics, even moving his headquarters out of Washington, D.C., to St. Louis, thereby limiting its influence in the important debates about the role of the army in the West.[78]

General William Tecumseh Sherman from the Brady-Handy Collection of the Library of Congress. Like most other generals in the West, Sherman distinguished himself in the Civil War, though he was often criticized for his "scorched earth" policy, particularly the "March to the Sea" through Georgia. Immediately after the war, he was appointed the commander of the Military Division of Missouri. Sherman became the commanding general of the U.S. Army in 1869 when Ulysses S. Grant assumed the presidency. Sherman would remain in that position until 1883. *Courtesy of the Library of Congress.*

Presidential administrations were often uninterested in Indian affairs as well. Even Grant, who showed more interest than most, quickly became uninterested after the "Indian Ring" scandals rocked his administration. Further complicating the situation was the ongoing debate about whether the military should be under civilian control of the secretary of war or the military control of the general of the army. The bickering at the top further complicated the formation of a clearly articulated policy.[79] Ideally, policies would have been clearly defined by the War Department and overseen by the president while incorporating views of interested parties, including reformers, agents and army personnel, not to mention perhaps representatives of the tribes themselves. Information would have flowed efficiently through a clearly defined chain of command, creating a deliberate, thoughtful and consistent policy that would be clearly articulated to field commanders and civilians.[80]

But no such ideal existed. To the contrary, the army had a dysfunctional structure of communication, held hostage by an ever-changing Congress that allocated funding, faced questions of ultimate leadership and was part of a larger debate about its role in American society. And even if a coherent policy could be formulated, the ability to communicate it was hampered by the technology of the time and bureaucratic structures of the army. The commanders were keenly aware of this. As Sheridan wrote to Brigadier General George Crook, "I am too far away to order or even suggest [a course of action]."[81] As a result, western Indian policy was left in limbo

This Is the Noble Red Man, from *Harper's Weekly*, December 21, 1878, demonstrating tension between government departments and personalities over U.S. Indian policy.

with no specific guidelines or clear directive, vacillating between "the rifle and the peace pipe."[82] As General Sherman explained it to Brevet Major General John Scholfield, the commander of the Department of Missouri in 1869, "The whole Indian Question is in such a snarl, that I am utterly powerless to help you by order or advice. Do the best you can."[83] Such confusion and lack of direction from the top would transfer down to post commanders in the field, leaving them without a clearly communicated policy to guide them. They faced pressures from many quarters, resulting in a certain level of frustration trying to implement inconsistent, unclear and conflicting policies that came down from on high through the chain of command.

So it was when the commanders of Fort Ellis faced the critical years in the mid-1870s at a time when several forces converged, bringing the Indian Wars to a climax in Montana. In the far distant aftermath of the Franco-Prussian War, Germany decided to go off the silver standard, causing a massive decline in the worldwide demand for silver. The economic ramifications trickled through the global economy causing the Panic of 1873 in the United States after the banking houses of Jay Cooke collapsed. The immediate consequences for the people of Montana were that the Northern Pacific Railroad, a syndicate of Cooke's, stopped its slow advance across the plains in Bismarck. The citizens of Bozeman had counted on the arrival of the railroad no later than 1873 to connect them with eastern markets as well as ridding the Yellowstone River Valley of bison, thereby minimizing the incursions of hostile tribes.[84] With rails stopped in Dakota, the populace of Bozeman resiliently decided to undertake an endeavor at "opening up communication with the Eastern States by way of the Yellowstone, [and] making connection with the Northern Pacific Railroad," even if that meant provoking a war with the Sioux and Northern Cheyenne.[85]

The plans began to form in the summer of 1873. It was clearly evident that a party of settlers heading down the Yellowstone to the mouth of the Big Horn River likely would be confronted by hostile bands of Sioux. The expedition gained momentum when J.L. Vernon brought the possibility of prospecting for gold.[86] Bozeman's J.V. Bogert admitted that, "without the Vernon idea, it must be admitted, the departure of the expedition would have been delayed."[87] The organizers asked Major Sweitzer, commander of Fort Ellis, if the military would stop their adventure. It was here that Sweitzer sought clarification, and as the months progressed, the danger seemed even more real. "If the movement goes on as is expected," Sweitzer wrote to his superiors in January 1874, "the result might be that the Government may be drawn into giving the Sioux a campaign that will forever settle the question of Indian hostilities."[88] Lieutenant General Sheridan responded that it would be "advisable" that they stay off the Crow Reservation.[89] It was also clear to the organizers that an Indian war might not only result from their actions but was actually desirable given military inaction:

> *It is possible the boys may precipitate difficulties and stir up a fight with the Indians…* [and] *make more Indians bite the dust in one round than the military have in the past five years…For if the hardy pioneers of the West were compelled to supinely wait on "military operations" to make the way into the rich mineral and agricultural regions clear of hostile Indians they would remain in their wild, inhabited state until doomsday.*[90]

The adventurers departed in early February 1874 and sent regular dispatches to the *Courier*. The commanders at Fort Ellis were given no directives to intervene so long as they stayed off the Crow Reservation. Later that month, members of the expedition were encouraged by the news of hostilities with the Sioux on the Red Cloud Agency, "as it relieves us of the responsibility of causing an Indian War."[91] Nearly a decade later, H.N. Maguire proudly boasted that the expedition had intentionally "precipitated the war against Sitting Bull" because of the army's "short-sighted policy," and he proudly claimed that it "expedited the extension of the railroad up the Yellowstone Valley and the general result is now seen in the chain of flourishing young cities."[92]

Major Sweitzer kept his superiors and the territorial governor apprised of the situation and claimed that no aid from Fort Ellis had been solicited.[93] It took months for the report to work its way through the chain of command and reach the secretary of the interior, who saw greater problems than Sheridan and wrote directly to Governor Potts, instructing him: "Oppose and prevent the departure…of this Expedition."[94] Potts, who had given moral and material support to the endeavor, responded that the expedition

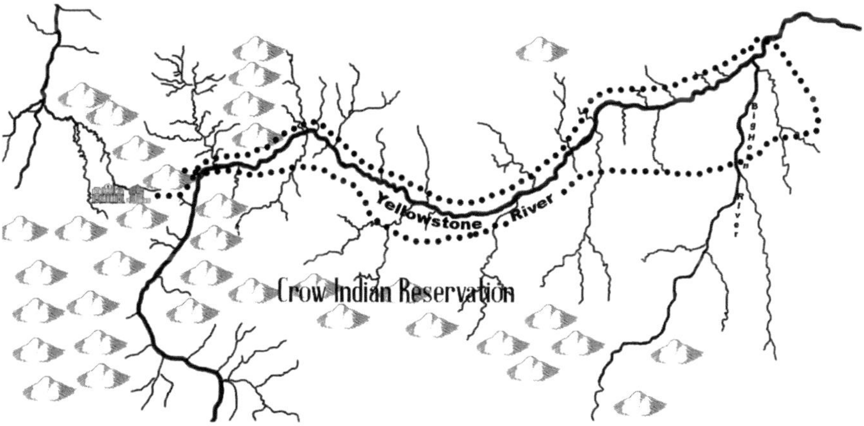

Yellowstone Wagonroad and Prospecting Expedition of 1874. *By author.*

had left months before assuming that Sheridan's advice to stay off the Crow Reservations "was the rule."[95]

Yet, the expedition members' spirits waned in the coming months under bad weather and increased Indian hostilities. By May, they had decided to return to Bozeman, but Bogert optimistically claimed, "It is not yet too late to save ourselves if we but go energetically to work to effect a reorganization" and began planning another expedition for the following year.[96] By the next January, Bogert began to drum up even more support "in view of the adverse report of the Senate Committee on the Northern Pacific Railroad bill" and claimed that "a united and determined effort should be made" to open the Yellowstone.[97] He claimed that "ridding the area of Indians" and bringing in the railroad was "a public necessity that the government cannot longer ignore."[98]

Again, the commanders of Fort Ellis inquired as to what their actions should be, particularly after the differing instructions they had received during the previous year's expedition. After being approached by one of the organizers, Captain D.W. Benham, temporarily commanding the fort and personally sympathetic to the Indians plight, responded that the organizer "was of the opinion that he will not be interfered with provided he does not trespass upon any of the Indian Reservation. On arriving at this conclusion I have been guided by the instructions given Major Sweitzer in regard to a similar expedition which started from here last year" but asked again for clarification.[99] Left only to offer an "opinion" and still needing clarification shows not only the uncertainty Benham was feeling but also his professionalism.

The new expedition left better prepared to face the hostilities it encountered. It arrived at the mouth of the Big Horn River near modern-day Custer, Montana, and erected a stockade christened Fort Pease. Reports of fighting streamed back for the rest of the summer and fall of 1875. The citizens of Bozeman tried to spur the government into action by asking it to come to the relief of the expedition. The post's new commander, Major James S. Brisbin, also generally sympathetic to the Native Americans, wired his commanders, keeping them informed and asking for instructions. "Citizens of Bozeman ask me to go to the relief of the men at Fort Pease," he wrote in February 1876. "Please instruct me what action I shall take."[100] The following day, Brisbin received his orders "to go at once to the relief of the men at Fort Pease."[101]

However, by the time Major Brisbin received his orders, the U.S. Army had been secretly planning and mobilizing for a major campaign against the Sioux in that region. Non-treaty bands had been ordered to return to their reservations by January 31, and when the deadline passed, General Sheridan

Protecting a Wagon Train, by Frederic Remington. *From* Drawings *(1897)*.

Cavalryman's Breakfast on the Plains, by Frederic Remington (1882).

officially ordered the commencement of hostilities on February 8, though the plan had been in the works for some time.[102] The presence of civilians in the middle of the field of operations would be problematic at best, and Brisbin may have forced some to return against their will.[103]

The Great Sioux War of 1876–77 followed by the Nez Perce War of 1877 clarified the mission of the U.S. Army in Montana. No longer were there confusing and vacillating orders coming from above, and the fear of civilians provoking an Indian war were inconsequential since the civilians were finally seeing the action they had so long desired. The army was like an unchained dog and took its mission with determination.[104] Surprisingly, the citizens of Bozeman still had issues with government policy. John Bogert claimed in a rather glib "I-told-you-so" tone that Lieutenant Colonel Custer's defeat at the Battle of the Little Big Horn was a "sad result no doubt brought about by the erroneous impression entertained by the government and many military leaders in under-estimating the strength of the Sioux Indians…which calls for immediate redress at the hands of the government and we don't think it can be accomplished by the present number of troops in the field."[105] Still, after the end of these conflicts, the military frontier remained generally peaceful despite some civilians' anxiety.[106] The commanders of Fort Ellis no longer found themselves with ambiguous or conflicting demands. In the end, while their frustrations may have made their responses inefficient, it did not make them ineffective, especially once the high command had committed them to a determined course of action.[107]

3
ECONOMIC RELATIONSHIP BETWEEN MILITARY AND CIVILIAN SOCIETY

Keep every dollar of this money at home.

On December 11, 1867, First Lieutenant John M. Green led a sixteen-man contingent of the Thirteenth United States Infantry to a small log cabin outside Bozeman, Montana. The occupants of the cabin had often enjoyed the visits of soldiers from the newly established Fort Ellis, constructed a few months earlier three miles east of Bozeman on the East Gallatin River. Most soldiers came to drink, undoubtedly providing a handsome profit for the owners. This visit was different, however. Lieutenant Green bore Special Order No. 39, issued by the commander of Fort Ellis, Captain Robert S. LaMotte. Episcopalian Bishop Daniel S. Tuttle described Captain LaMotte as "an uncompromising total abstainer" to the point that many of the officers under his command, "were not all together comfortable" with his position on alcohol.[108] LaMotte's orders to Green were clear. He was to:

> *Pull down said log house…It having come to the knowledge* [of] *the commanding officer that persons occupying said house are in the habit of furnishing the soldiers of this post with intoxicating liquor, although repeatedly warned that such conduct would not he permitted.*[109]

Three days later, Captain LaMotte carried his war directly into the town of Bozeman itself when he sent a contingent of twelve soldiers:

Arresting the Deserter, by Frederic Remington, 1885.

> *To the business place of a certain person, known by the name of "Colonel Chestnut," located in the town of Bozeman City and there confiscate and destroy all spirituous and alcoholic liquors he may find on the premises. From there he will proceed to the house, on the door east of Fuller & Rich's store…known as "The Saloon" and likewise confiscate, pour out and destroy all intoxicating liquors he may find.*[110]

LaMotte's war against these Bozeman establishments was an early example of the ambivalent economic relations between the military society at Fort Ellis and the civilian society at Bozeman. Military forts have provided economic stimuli to local civilian settlements throughout history. Providing goods for soldiers and supplies for the fort increased the flow of money into the local economies. In sparsely settled regions such as the American West, this economic input was especially critical to civilian settlements. In Montana, posts such as Fort Ellis in the Gallatin Valley brought much-needed money during a critical stage of settlement in the area, particularly for the main population center of Bozeman. Like many other military towns in the West, the embryonic settlement of Bozeman depended on the fort to provide economic security that ensured its growth and survival until westward expansion of the railroads gave access to distant markets. Nevertheless, the military and town often found themselves in economic conflict with each other based on these economic relations.

Fort Ellis and Bozeman provide a localized example of how tensions and conflict arose in an often-tempestuous relationship of civilian and military economic interdependence. For the community, this tension was both internal (that is, between civilians in competition for economic resources the fort provided) and external (between the civilians and the military). At times, civilians, consciously aware of the economic potential of the fort, perfidiously took advantage of the post's dollars, adding to tension between the town and the fort. In a type of frontier mercantilism, Bozeman's businessmen acted both honestly and dishonestly to draw hard currency from the federal government into the local economy. Nevertheless, the economic input caused agitation in addition to needed economic stimuli.

The excitement of the militia's "Montana Picnic" was starting to subside when the regular army arrived in August 1867. The army more than

Main Street in Bozeman, facing west, circa 1860s. A wooden bridge lies in the foreground of the image, spanning Sourdough Creek. Two blacksmith shops stand at the right of the dirt street behind the bridge. The LaClede Hotel is visible at right with the flag flying above it. *Courtesy of the Gallatin County Historical Society.*

doubled the number of people living in the eastern edge of the Gallatin Valley. Bozeman citizens, fewer than one hundred strong, used Fort Ellis as a new market for their goods. As travel over the Bozeman Trail gradually slowed and then ceased, the soldiers at the new post replaced the monetary flow that trail migrants had previously provided. The town gave the soldiers opportunities for relief from the monotony of garrison life. The whiskey, women and material goods relieved the loneliness of the frontier soldier. On the official level, the town also furnished manpower and supplies that the post needed.

The economic input provided by the military came at a time when two forces were converging and bringing a bleak outlook for Bozeman and the Gallatin Valley. The closure of the Bozeman Trail to migrant traffic and the dollars those immigrants brought spelled problems for the merchants of the town. In addition, agricultural overproduction and gradual decline in the mining population created a drop in the price of agricultural staples, making farming problematic even in the very fertile Gallatin Valley. The fort's payroll and demand for supplies helped alleviate these conditions to an extent and gave Bozeman an element of economic security.

When Captain Robert S. LaMotte began construction of Fort Ellis in the fall of 1867, "private labor" provided most of the manpower for constructing the buildings—that is, the privates and enlisted men furnished the labor. Because LaMotte's two companies of the Thirteenth Infantry started work late in the year, they did not complete all the buildings before winter started to set in. By December of that year, LaMotte found it necessary to hire local civilians to help finish the construction. He directed his quartermaster to employ "a sufficient number of teams to haul logs to be used in the erection of quarters and other buildings…These teams become necessary as the government teams…are constantly employed hauling wood, water, sand, adobes, and poles." The weather was his foremost concern as he stressed that "the season is now far advanced and no time is to be lost to get the necessary logs and timber from the mountain before winter sets in and the woods become impassible."[111]

The employment of men in constructing buildings at the fort did not end when the fort was completed. The major maintenance and expansion of the fort required skilled carpenters and laborers. Citizens looked forward to such improvements since the employment of local men would invigorate the local economy. An 1873 edition of the *Bozeman Avant Courier* cheerfully stated that "improvements at Fort Ellis are being pushed with a vim…We understand that in a few weeks, 50 additional workmen will be employed on the new

Company F, Second Cavalry, at Fort Ellis in 1874. Note the condition of the long building in the background. Exactly which building is pictured is not known, but compare the condition of the building with the description by the *Avant Courier* the same year. *Courtesy of the Gallatin County Historical Society.*

buildings at Ellis."[112] By 1874, the deterioration of the original log buildings became so severe that the army considered replacing all or most of the log buildings with new framed ones. With obvious excitement, the *Courier* ran the following article:

> *General Sheridan having favorably reported the proposed new buildings to substitute the old ones at Fort Ellis another year will probably see a suitable military post erected near the present inadequate and decaying structures. The new post, it is estimated, will involve the expenditure of $200,000 or more.*[113]

The plan to build an almost completely new fort did not come about. However, refurbishing of the existing buildings did occur. New building projects included the covering of the original log structures with planking, expanding some buildings, razing others and erecting new ones. The blueprints and plans of the fort show how older buildings changed or disappeared while new ones arose.

The constant maintenance of the buildings as well as other tasks at the fort required semipermanent employment of a limited number of civilians. Merrill Burlingame noted that it was difficult to secure adequate statements of the total cost for employing civilians since assorted accounts were separately handled.[114] Yet a report of Lieutenant Colonel Samuel B. Holabird on his trip through the Military Department of Dakota detailed some of the civilian labor costs at Fort Ellis in 1869. Holabird listed six carpenters, one blacksmith and one guide, each paid $75.00 annually, as well as one

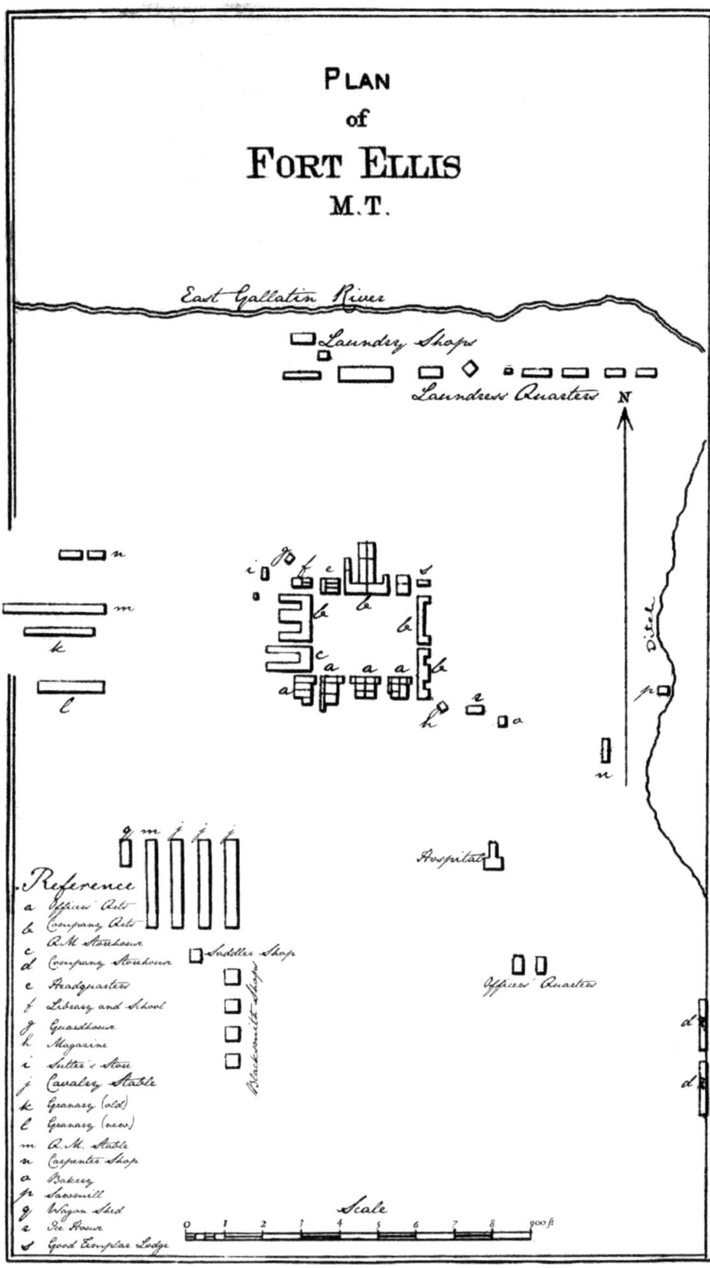

Plan of Fort Ellis, 1876. Compare with the images on page 27 and 55, which show how buildings changed over the lifespan of the fort. *From* Outline Descriptions of the Posts in the Military Division of the Missouri *(1876)*. (Image modified for clarity and legibility.)

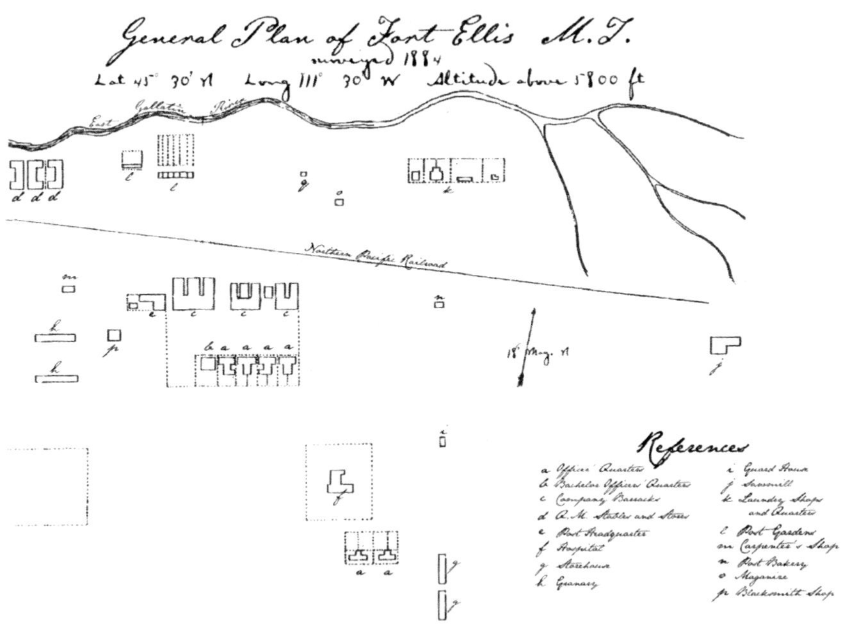

Plan of Fort Ellis, 1884. The orientation of the plan is opposite of the images on page 27 and 54. Note that the Northern Pacific Railroad tracks are located between the barracks and the East Gallatin River. *Courtesy of Renne Library Special Collections, Montana State University, Bozeman, Montana. (Image modified for clarity and legibility.)*

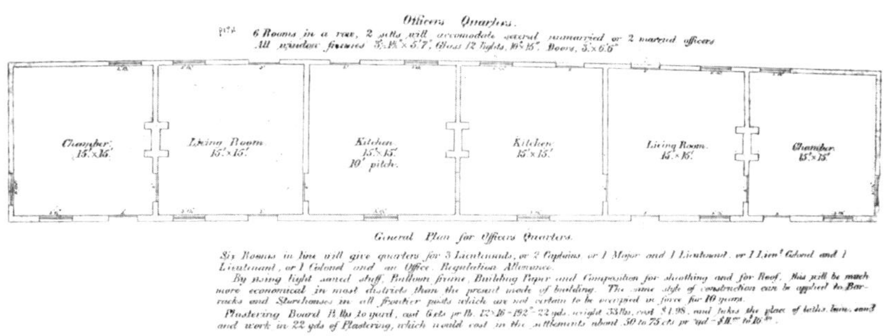

Supposed blueprints of the officers' quarters at Fort Ellis drawn in 1876. The plans, however, show little resemblance to photographs of the officers' quarter in the image on page 92 when the fort was still active and on page 56 after the fort was abandoned. In both cases, there is a gabled entrance that protrudes behind the front, making the structure T shaped. The plans of the fort from 1868, 1876 and 1884 show this as well and suggest that these plans may be generic military plan for quarters but never actually implemented at the post. *Courtesy of Renne Library Special Collections, Montana State University, Bozeman, Montana.*

Photo of the abandoned officers' quarters after 1886. The buildings remain a combination of log and clapboard. Again, note how the photo does not conform to the supposed plans in the previous image. Even the junior officers' quarters to the far right, which do not appear to be T shaped, still do not conform in proportion to the plans or the number of windows and presumably rooms or to the plans of the fort in 1868, 1876 or 1884. *Courtesy of the Gallatin County Historical Society.*

clerk and one engineer, each paid $125.00 annually. The fort also paid $24,782.13 for hired mule and ox teams to augment the military teams and another $35,261.23 for material and short-term labor. However, he also noted that several items were overpaid and "indicates that little discretion in such matters can safely be given to officers generally."[115]

When the military engaged in maneuvers, the need for short-term contracted labor sometimes increased. In the summer of 1872, many of the soldiers from the fort headed toward the Yellowstone River Valley to patrol and protect the Northern Pacific Railroad surveying crew. The post teamsters and wagons that usually engaged in bringing supplies to the fort left with them. Captain L. Cass Forsyth, the acting post quartermaster, hired six civilian teamsters to "haul the post lumber that had been purchased from various mills for the public buildings now in the process of erection."[116] Depending on the time of year, the civilian teamsters could raise the price for their services. Lieutenant McAdams, the assistant post quartermaster, informed the acting post commander that "teamsters could not be hired for less than 40 or 50 dollars a month" during the late summer and early fall harvest.[117]

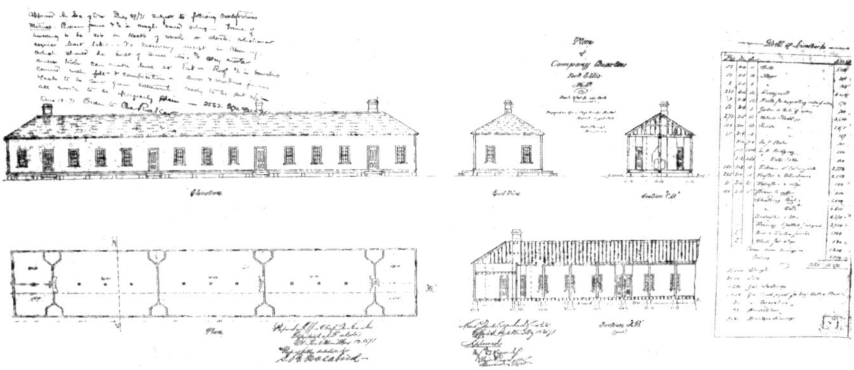

Supposed plans for company quarters at Fort Ellis. Like the plans for the officers' quarters, these plans do not conform to photographs of the quarters in the following image and overall fort plans (pages 27, 54 and 55), which indicate that there are several perpendicular wings that protrude from behind the front of the quarters. The total board feet required to build the structure is estimated on the image as 51,876. *Courtesy of Renne Library Special Collections, Montana State University, Bozeman, Montana.*

Photo of abandoned company quarters after 1886. The building appears with clapboards, different than the images on page 53 and above, which show buildings built with logs. The clapboard may cover the log superstructure here or the building may be a framed building as the blueprints would suggest. However, the building does not generally conform to the blueprints as the perpendicular wings present in the overall for plans appear visible in this photo but not on the blueprints for the company quarters. *Courtesy of the Gallatin County Historical Society.*

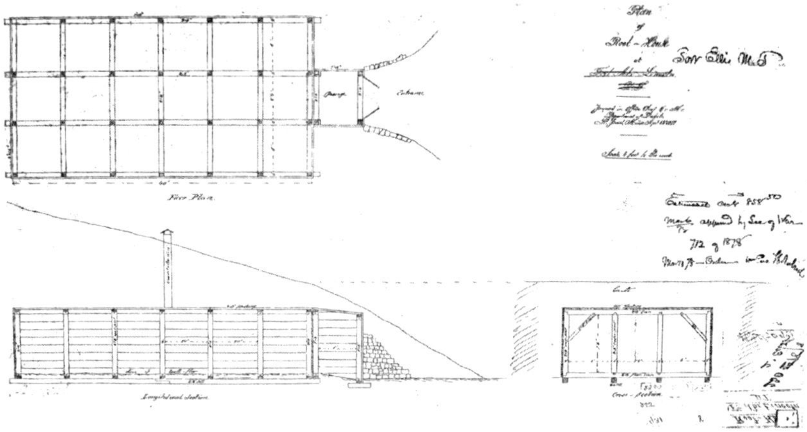

A blueprint for the root cellar at Fort Ellis. There is no known photograph of it, but these plans may indicate why the other blueprints do not conform to the photographic evidence of other buildings. Note that the words "Fort Abraham Lincoln" have been crossed out and the words "Fort Ellis" added. This suggests that the blueprints may be rather generic in nature, and the plans for the company quarters do in fact appear similar to the quarters at Fort Abraham Lincoln near modern-day Bismarck, North Dakota. Thus, while the plans may have been meant to be applied to Fort Ellis, that does not necessarily mean they actually were. *Courtesy of Renne Library Special Collections, Montana State University, Bozeman, Montana.*

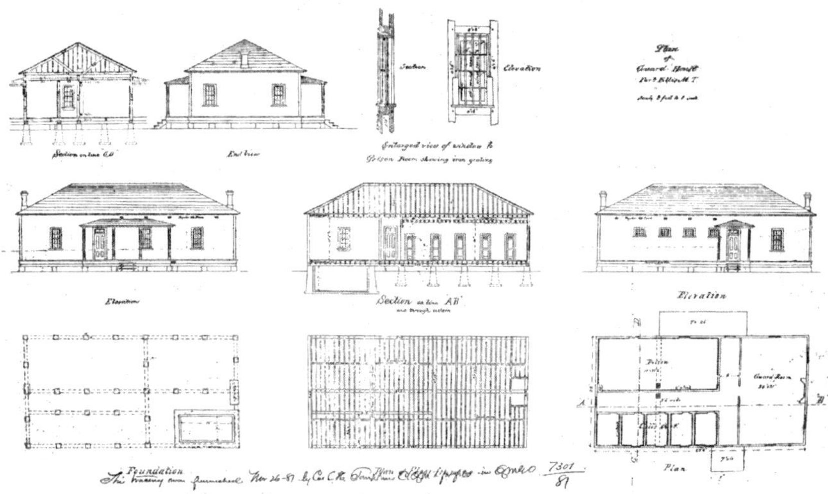

Plan for the guardhouse at Fort Ellis. In this case, the plan does conform to the photographic evidence, as the top image on the following page shows similarities to the building, at least on the outside. *Courtesy of Renne Library Special Collections, Montana State University, Bozeman, Montana.*

Photograph of the abandoned guardhouse at Fort Ellis, sometime after 1886. This does appear to conform to the blueprint of the structure. *Courtesy of the Gallatin County Historical Society.*

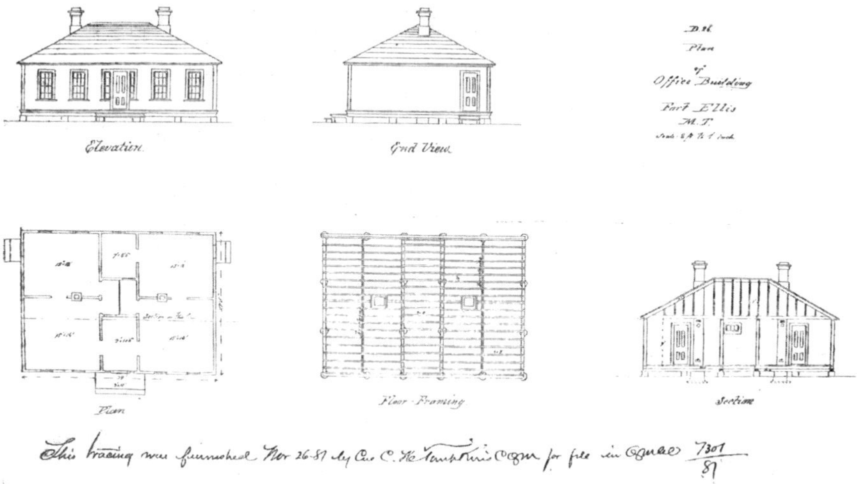

A blueprint for the office building at Fort Ellis. It is not clear if the actual office building conformed to this plan. *Courtesy of Renne Library Special Collections, Montana State University, Bozeman, Montana.*

Railroad Building on the Great Plains, from *Harper's Weekly*, July 17, 1875. Troops across the West, including those at Fort Ellis, played a major role in protecting surveying and construction parties for the railroad companies. General Sherman strongly supported the spreading of the railroad across the West as a means to pacify the military situation. The troops from Fort Ellis were particularly crucial in the Northern Pacific Railroad's advancement down the Yellowstone River Valley as the rails moved west from Bismarck, North Dakota.

Besides the official government employees, some citizens of Bozeman became privately employed as domestic servants for officers' families. How much these people were paid is unknown, as their services were privately arranged. Until 1872, enlisted men could be employed by the officers as servants called "strikers." By 1872, official army policy discouraged this activity because it distracted the soldiers from their official duties.[118] After that, the officers hired local civilians. The census records for Fort Ellis show four civilian domestic servants in 1870 and nine in 1880. Frances Roe, wife of First Lieutenant Fayette Washington Roe, hired at least three servants, usually Chinese, while posted in Montana.[119]

When the decision was made to create a post on the upper part of the Bozeman Trail, some military officials felt that it would be strategically more sound to locate the fort on the east side of the Bozeman Pass. This, after all, was the direction from which the Indians would come, and the fort location would enable easier patrolling of the Yellowstone Valley. However, citizens of Bozeman pointed out that the fertile Gallatin Valley could more easily supply a fort located on the west side of the pass.[120] The supply of frontier posts was no small concern to military officials. Department commanders took care to locate posts in strategically advantageous positions and in places where local products would supply as much of the garrison's needs as possible.[121] Consequently, the army built the fort three miles from Bozeman on the west side of the Bozeman Pass.

Frontier posts in Montana had a large number of soldiers to feed. The daily rations were as routine and monotonous as the usual round of garrison duties. Lieutenant Colonel C.G. Gilbert of Fort Shaw described the army rations for troopers in Montana as consisting of

> *twelve ounces of pork or Bacon or one pound four ounces of salt or fresh beef, one pound two ounces of soft bread of flour or one pound hard bread or one pound four ounces of corn meal and to every one-hundred* [men] *a ration of fifteen pounds of beans or peas or ten pounds of rice or hominy, ten pounds of green coffee or eight pounds of roasted (or roasted and ground) coffee or one pound and eight ounces of tea, fifteen pounds of sugar, four quarts of vinegar, one pound four ounces of adamantine or star candles, four pounds of soap, three pounds twelve ounces of salt and four ounces of pepper.*[122]

Fresh vegetables were not traditionally included in the rations issued to soldiers, but the army recognized the need for proper nutrition. The raising of company gardens was strongly encouraged and became a source of pride and competition among companies at a post.[123] Because of the fertile soil around Fort Ellis, a garden of 26.5 acres produced a large amount of fresh vegetables. In 1879, Major Brisbin estimated the value of the vegetables raised equal to $7,182. The amount of vegetables grown that year included:

> *3,865 bushels of potatoes*
> *336 bushels of onions*
> *785 bushels of turnips*
> *172 bushels of carrots*
> *105 bushels of beets*
> *75 bushels of parsnips*
> *12,500 heads of cabbage.*[124]

Supplies other than vegetables needed to be obtained from local sources. Staples such as flour, grain, beef and pork were needed for human consumption, and the cavalry's horses needed straw, oats and hay. In addition, coal and cordwood were needed for heat in the winter. The farmers and citizens of Bozeman and the Gallatin Valley were pleased to supply the needed items.

Montana agriculture had entered a slump in the mid- to late 1860s as production increased and prices dropped. Many miners became discouraged with sluicing for gold and began to farm for a living. The Gallatin Valley, by far the most fertile area in the territory at that time, became a likely destination for the disheartened miners. The addition of these new farmers and the continued expansion of existing farms created a yield explosion in the last half of the 1860s. In 1865, the valley produced 20,000 bushels of wheat. Two years later, some estimated that the valley produced 300,000 bushels of wheat raised on 8,351 acres of land. The figure of 300,000 might be a little high, because the 1870 census listed only 180,000 bushels of wheat raised.[125]

The dramatic increase of production that exceeded the growth of the territory's population forced a drop in prices for wheat and flour. Burlingame noted that, according to the *Montana Post*, the price of flour dropped from twenty-five to forty dollars a sack in 1865 to eight to fifteen dollars a sack in 1868. Unground wheat dropped from ten dollars a bushel in 1865 to two dollars a bushel in 1871. The seven flourmills in the territory, four of which were located around Bozeman, produced all the flour the territory needed.[126]

The Bozeman and Gallatin Valley farmers were more than pleased to have a new market for their goods. The process of bidding for the fort's contracts originally involved having only approved speculators bid on the proposals. These speculators would then fill their obligations by purchasing the grain and other items from the local farmers, keeping a modest profit for themselves. Since the speculators could more economically fill their contracts from local rather than distant farmers, the speculators each counted on the same farmers. Therefore, no matter who was awarded the contracts, the farmers received a certain share of the proceeds.

Yet the citizens of the valley felt that by eliminating the speculators, more money would remain in the local economy. In 1870, the military decided to allow individual citizens to bid on the contracts. The editor of the *Montana Pick and Plow*, the predecessor to the *Bozeman Avant Courier*, commented:

> *Now the farmers and businessmen of this valley can, just as well as not cut off the "middle-men" or foreign speculators, and keep every dollar of this*

> *money at home...There is no necessity of allowing speculators to have the use of your money without paying the usual rate of four percent a month, a single hour.*[127]

Still, the process was stacked against the local farmers since they could not always meet the quantity or prices that the speculators offered. The *Pick and Plow* editor proposed a system by which the local farmers could form a collective to undermine the speculators:

> *By combination and mutual understanding, control the whole business. Put everything down at the most reasonable figures, declaring the lowest figures at which the next crops can be produced—bearing in mind that there will be future contracts to fill, and that self-interest will be subserved* [sic] *by making a favorable impression on the War Department through the pending transactions...Let the valley be divided into districts, for the consideration of this matter...let a day then be appointed for the various committees to meet in Bozeman, for general conference and the selection of representative must undertake the business as a matter of* public spirit, not personal speculation, *and be satisfied with reasonable compensation.*[128]

The attempt to rid the process of foreign speculators was only partially successful. The *Courier* files show that a greater number of small farmers and contractors brought supplies to Fort Ellis. Yet large-scale contracting along the old lines of the foreign speculator still persisted with a few foreign speculators and some of the town patriarchs filling the role of a speculator. Lester S. Willson, Daniel Rouse, P.W. McAdow, Achilles Lamme, J.S. Mendenhall, William Tracy, Nelson Story and Lester M. Black were involved in this activity. People such as Nelson Story had an advantage in

A photo of Nelson Story taken around 1893. *Courtesy of Renne Library Special Collections, Montana State University, Bozeman, Montana.*

RES. OF NELSON STORY, BOZEMAN, GALLATIN CO.

VALLEY MILL, NELSON STORY, PROPRIETOR, BOZEMAN, GALLATIN CO.

Residence and mill owned by Nelson Story. Story had diverse economic interests in Bozeman and the Gallatin Valley. The modest house shown was later replaced by a large Neo-Gothic mansion located where the former Wilson School, now the administrative building for School District 7, currently is located. *From Michael Leeson's* History of Montana *(1885).*

competing for post contracts. His diverse interests in farming, ranching, freighting and mercantilism gave him sufficient capital to offer a lower bid for supplies and then purchase any excess stores from smaller farmers to fulfill his quotas.

The exact amounts of supplies and bids offered are hard to ascertain. The *Courier* often listed the amount rendered by contractors but not the amount the military required. One exception was in March 1872. On March 14, the *Courier* listed the amount of hay needed by the fort as 923 tons, straw as 284 tons and 1,864 cords of wood. Two weeks later, on March 28, the *Courier* listed the bids tendered as follows:[129]

BIDDER	HAY	STRAW	WOOD
B. McCall	$—	$—	$5.90
John Mitchell	$19.90	$—	$—
McAdow Bros.	$29.75	$9.00	$—
Robert Walling Ford	$—	$—	$6.40
R.S. McDonald	$18.80	$8.00	$—
Chas. Rich	$7.00	$8.00	$—
Burnack	$19.80	$19.00	$—
Casper	$16.75	$—	$6.35
Lockey	$17.75	$8.25	$1.95

The amount of profit is difficult to estimate since the cost of production is unknown. Yet assuming the army took the lowest bids for each category, Charles Rich would have grossed $6,461.00 for his hay bid, either R.S. McDonald or Charles Rich would have grossed $2,272.00 for their bids on the straw, and B. McCall would have grossed $10,997.60 for his bid on the wood.

Because of the location of Fort Ellis in the productive Gallatin Valley and its proximity to the Yellowstone River Valley, it became the supply center for the Crow Indian Agency thirty miles to the east and Fort Keogh and Fort Custer, two new posts established after the Sioux War of 1876. Since the new forts were in nonarable land that also lacked lumber for construction, maintenance and fuel, Bozeman profited from an increased military demand for goods. For example, in 1879, Fort Custer required 250,000 pounds of oats, a contract won by R.S. McDonald with a bid of $3.80 a pound, grossing $950,000.00.[130]

View of Bozeman's main street looking east in the early 1870s. Notice the brick Metropolitan hotel in background on the left and the large brick building under construction, known as the Cooper and Black building, on the south side of the street. This dates the photo to the early 1870s as the building was completed in 1872. It housed the armory and gun manufacturing facility of William Cooper and the general store of Lester Black. The Young Men's Library Association was on the second floor. Brick buildings required greater investment and had the symbolic importance of demonstrating the determination of the citizens to make the settlement a success. *Courtesy of the Gallatin County Historical Society.*

Freighting supplies for the contractors became almost as lucrative as being a contractor for the forts. The large quantity of supplies required by Fort Ellis alone caused the *Avant Courier* to proclaim: "Our streets have presented a lively appearance the past few days. The arrival of trains with goods and transit of those supplying the Fort with hay, grain, &c, keep the streets almost blocked."[131]

No matter who received the contracts for supplying the fort, a contractor could reap the benefits. Individual farmers, particularly the smaller ones, did not have the equipment or manpower to haul the large quantities efficiently and had to hire out their work to professional freighters. Regardless of who won the contracts, the freighters had work. William (Billy) Frazier claimed he "had to quit farming and go into freighting" to make a more steady living. "Because of the low prices involved in farming during the early seventies,"

Billy Frazier professed that "farmers had a hard time making a living in the Gallatin Valley" despite its abundant agricultural yields.[132]

The citizens of Bozeman not only enjoyed the economic benefit of the fort but also outright expected the fort to aid them economically. The fear of losing the fort's contracts was clearly evident to the citizens of Bozeman on at least two occasions that demonstrated how they viewed the economic importance of the fort. Some citizens became agitated when they merely suspected that the fort was securing flour from outside sources without rendering local contracts. Their suspicions started in May 1871 when a wagon train of supplies, including several sacks of flour, came through town headed to the fort. The editor of the *Courier* wondered in a rather accusatory tone "why flour should be imported from St. Louis at a cost of $9 per hundred when as good an article can be had in this country for $2 per hundred in any quantity desired." He also requested that a representative of the government explain why the fort had not called for bids. "We wish for the sake of our farmers, who have no market for the large crops of this year, that they would."[133]

In the next issue of the *Courier*, Lieutenant James G. MacAdams, the post quartermaster, wrote and explained the fort's position. He claimed that there were only one hundred sacks of flour, specially ordered by certain officers of the post with their own private money. He reassured the residents of Bozeman that this did not affect the usual contracts. The *Courier* consequently apologized for insinuating that Lieutenant MacAdams had acted incorrectly and acknowledged that MacAdams "is our good friend and uses every effort to have all supplies purchased in this market."[134] Clearly, despite historian Frederick Jackson Turner's seminal thesis that the rugged frontier environment forced each generation of Americans to "rebuild" American society free from the constraints of eastern civilization, the citizens of Bozeman were not rebuilding themselves free from the eastern federal government. Rather, they saw it as the duty of the government, as exemplified by Fort Ellis, to help them build their community.

Fort Ellis became a vital link in the supply line of the "Montana Column" that included troops from Fort Shaw, Camp Baker and Fort Ellis during the Great Sioux War of 1876. The extraordinary demands of prolonged campaigning exhausted the local market of some items. While sending grain to the troops in the field, the army needed an unusually high number of grain sacks, more than Bozeman could supply. Special Order No. 62, dated May 13, 1876, directed the quartermaster "to purchase on the open market at Helena, there being none in Bozeman markets, one-hundred and fifty (150) grain sacks required by troops in the field from this post."[135]

The demands of the Sioux War, particularly following Lieutenant Colonel (Brevet Major General) George A. Custer's defeat, created a need for higher troop levels in the area. The troops stationed at Fort Ellis at the end of 1875 numbered 288. By the end of 1876, the number had increased to 449.[136] The increase of soldiers brought expanded consumption of supplies, and the farmers and merchants undoubtedly benefitted from this windfall of the Indian wars. Special arrangements had to be made for some supplies as the increased demand on stores grew. The commissary that sold meat to officers and their families had to arrange for the officers to purchase their meat from local butchers. The commanding officer made it clear that "this arrangement is necessary at the present time owing to the disproportion existing between enlisted men and officer families to be supplied." He assured the officers that the contractor would supply equal amounts of all meat at ten cents per pound.[137]

The next distressing event for Bozemanites came when the military became embroiled in the partisan politics of Washington, D.C., during the final years of Reconstruction in the South. When the Democrats gained control of the House of Representatives in 1875, they engaged in a four-year effort to reduce the military, a strong and ever-present symbol of Republican efforts at Reconstruction in the South. Adding fuel to the flames was President Ulysses S. Grant's deployment of troops at polling places in the South during the presidential election of 1876. The hostility the Democrats harbored toward the military came to a head when the 1877 army appropriation bill became locked in a seesaw battle between the Democratic House and the Republican Senate in an effort to reduce the size of the army. A last-ditch effort to remedy the situation failed before Congress adjourned in March 1877. At the end of the fiscal year in June, the army ceased to receive pay.[138]

Partisan politics compounded with the military actions of 1876 and 1877 also confronted the army with an unexpected lack of funds. The defeat of Custer came as a surprise, and not enough money had been appropriated for the fiscal year. A rumor about this situation found its way into the pages of the *Courier*, and the possible withdrawal of the fort market greatly concerned the residents of the area. The bids had already been submitted, but it was rumored that they would be "re-advertised and re-bid upon...This course would seem just to bidders...but must result in dangerous delays affecting both contractor and the service."[139] The fort responded by confirming the rumors and furnishing a telegram from the chief quartermaster of the army, stating that "no contracts for supplies for the army pertaining to the

HOSTILE—BUT ACCOMMODATING.

UNCLE SAM—"*Wait until Congress meets, and then I'll settle your account.*"
HOSTILE—"*Just send your army up my way, and I'll reduce it without waiting for Congress.*"

A political cartoon entitled *Hostile—But Accommodating*, from *Frank Leslie's Illustrated Newspaper*, September 1, 1877. Uncle Sam is asking the Indian at the window to "wait until Congress meets, and then I will settle your account." The "hostile" replies, "Just send your army my way, and I'll reduce it without waiting for Congress." The Army Reduction Act caused great concern in towns like Bozeman, not only from the concern about protection from Indians but also for the ability to have the army to infuse the local economy with government funds.

Quartermaster Department for the fiscal year commencing July 1, 1877, will be made until the necessary appropriations have been made to pay for the same."[140] For the settlers in the Gallatin Valley, the main concern was how payment for supplies to Fort Ellis would be affected by this situation. The importance of the money that military contracts contributed to the local economy was obvious to the citizens.

There was also great concern among locals when contractors conspired to keep money for themselves at the expense of other settlers in the area. In 1871, a "foreign" speculator named J.V. Bogert withheld payment to farmers for their grain and directed them to collect goods "in kind" at the store of Willson & Rich instead. The editor of the *Avant Courier* felt it was wrong to compel farmers to "purchase at this house, when it was their custom and desire to purchase at other merchants."[141] The conspiracy that the *Courier* implied threatened to drive other businesses into hard times if one of the major money sources in the valley were funneled to one establishment and just a few citizens. He claimed that Fort Ellis:

> *Affords a market for the products of this valley, and from that source ranchmen expect to get money to pay their debts and make future purchases. Just so long as they are kept waiting for that money, just so long is the general prosperity of our people affected. The money received by them passes through the hands of every man in the county enabling all to pay their obligations. This is one of the main reasons assigned by many for the unusual scarcity of money in Gallatin County this season.*[142]

Bogert responded in the next issue, demanding an immediate retraction of the *Courier*'s allegations, but the editor replied that the newspaper reported only a rumor of such an agreement and refused to issue an apology. Bogert asserted that the article was slanderous and vowed to have signed affidavits to prove that such an arrangement did not exist. He claimed to have "disbursed here over $70,000—not one cent of which has been goods of any kind…It has been my desire to establish…so good a name that nothing done or attempted by me can justify or affect either 'my character' or 'good standing' as a stranger among you." Bogert did not leave Bozeman. In fact, he stayed in the area and became the town's first mayor. By all accounts, he is still considered one of the town's patriarchs and has a city park named for him. That in no way implies Bogert's innocence, however. In 1940, a Works Progress Administration (WPA) oral history interview with the pioneer freighter Billy Frazier confirmed that Bogert had indeed directed his debtors to the Willson & Rich establishment, where Bogert became a partner two years later.[143]

Occasionally, contractors not only acted less than honestly with farmers and other locals but also behaved dishonestly when dealing with the fort. The military was, in fact, acutely aware of dishonestly fulfilling contracts at Fort Ellis. In 1870, Lieutenant Colonel Samuel B. Holabird questioned the bids submitted for grain. He noted that "grain ought to cost not over 5 cents per pound, and hay about $15 per ton" but added that recent purchases "in this country cost from 300 to 500 percent above Chicago and St. Louis prices...[with] 500,000 pounds of grain, [purchased] at 10 cents per pound; and 300 tons of hay, at $32.50 per ton." He also noted that the delivered grain was below the quantity paid and laid responsibility at the foot of the army officers. "Only 300,000 pounds of grain were delivered. In my opinion, this purchase was a very bad one, and indicates little discretion in such matters can safely be given to officers general."[144] To prove his point of the officers' incompetence and the contractor's dishonesty, he noted that another later contract for 1,000,000 pounds of grain was delivered to Fort Ellis "at an average rate of four cents and one-tenth mills per pound, and 125 tons of hay at $16.74 per ton."[145]

According to Malcolm Story, his grandfather, the influential businessman and town patriarch Nelson Story, committed outright fraud when selling horses to Fort Ellis. When the army wanted to purchase several hundred horses, Story showed the inspectors fifty to one hundred horses that he

Photograph of Fort Parker (the first Crow Agency) facing northeast, photographed by William Henry Jackson in 1871. The Crow Indian Agency was established in 1868 under the terms of the Fort Laramie Treaty. Fort Parker, to the east of the present-day airport at Livingston, Montana, was constructed in 1869 to encourage the Crow Tribe to live a more sedentary lifestyle. In 1875, the agency moved to a site near present-day Absarokee, Montana. *Courtesy of the National Park Service Archives.*

claimed were representative of his stock. The officers wanted to inspect more examples of this herd and asked to see some additional horses. Story reportedly told his foreman to "run them around the hill again" and showed the officers the same horses they had already seen. When the sale was finally made, the balance of the remaining six hundred horses was below the quality of those originally shown to the inspectors.[146] This story is more than likely exaggerated or perhaps even completely untrue "whiskey talk." The annual reports of the secretary of war do not indicate that such a sale ever took place during the history of the fort. True or not, it illustrates the fact that the settlers had no objections to—and perhaps were even proud of—obtaining military money dishonestly.

Nelson Story was in fact formally accused of fraudulent dealings on his Crow Indian contracts. The Crow Reservation consisted of all the land in the territory south of the Yellowstone River and west of the forty-third meridian. Fort Ellis had a major role in the administration of the reservation. Billy Frazier, a freighter for Nelson Story, flatly asserted that Story had been openly fraudulent in fulfilling his government contracts, "but so would any of the rest of us who had the chance he did." He added, "We all thought that any smart man should steal from the Indians in those days." When presented with the opportunity, Frazier even personally aided Story in defrauding the Crows. For example, when he was hauling oats to the agency, it started to rain. He uncovered the oats and let them become soaked. When he arrived at the agency, his eight-thousand-pound cargo weighed eleven thousand pounds, a difference that equated to ninety dollars, which he offered to split with Nelson Story.[147]

The most sensational accusation against Story concerned his pork shipments to the Crow Agency in 1875 and 1876. Those shipments brought him into direct conflict with officers at the post. Captain Edward Ball of the Second Cavalry, stationed at Fort Ellis, was the inspector of Story's pork shipments. Ball reported that Story's pork:

> *Consisted of the entire hog, head and feet included and could not come under the head of mess pork as required by the terms of the contract and I rejected* [it]. *I would then state that that portion of the pork belonging to mess pork was of good quality and would have passed the inspection had it been packed separately but the entire head, shoulders, backbone, and tail with all the trimmings from the hams were also packed with it which in my judgment was good cause for rejecting the entire lot.*[148]

Ball further alleged that Nelson Story offered to give him $1,000 to approve the pork shipment. Story also proposed that some grain that he was to supply, but that had not yet arrived, be counted as received and the profits be divided among himself, Ball and the Crow agent Dexter Clapp. Captain Ball adamantly refused. In addition, Ball also believed that Story had "double-sacked" his previous flour shipments. During inspection, a bag of flour would be stamped received and then recorded. If double sacked, after inspection, the outer sack could be removed and the second sack stamped again and counted a second time. Ball's allegations went before a grand jury at the district court in Virginia City. The jury returned no charges, causing the presiding judge to reprimand them for not doing their duty because the evidence clearly favored an indictment.[149]

Perhaps the most frequent and visible economic exchange between the settlers and the soldiers happened on a much smaller scale, mainly the exchange of goods and services between individual soldiers and merchants, businessmen or other entrepreneurs. Even in this small-scale exchange, civilians could be equally as enterprising to take advantage of the situation and maximize their gain. Almost immediately after Captain R.S. LaMotte founded Fort Ellis in 1867, the merchants of Bozeman started to capitalize on the soldier's pay. The town provided goods and services that offered the soldiers a break in the routine of garrison duty. The soldiers provided a new market for merchants to replace the one lost when the government closed the Bozeman Trail. On three separate occasions, William White described "doing justice to a well supplied table."[150] The appetizing food and relaxation in town became especially comforting after he returned from a long patrol in the Yellowstone Valley.[151]

The town was such a draw for the soldiers that trips to town frequently interfered with the soldiers' military duties and became problematic for the post commanders, who strove at least to regulate the excursions. On December 7 of that year, Major James Brisbin issued general Order No. 55, which stated:

> *It having been reported to the commanding officer that enlisted men of this command are in the habit of visiting the town of Bozeman without permission; all such persons are warned to at once desist from this practice or they will be considered as absent without leave and treated accordingly.*[152]

Still, Brisbin realized that the town provided a morale boost to the soldier engaged in the unexciting work of garrison duty: "The post commander favors the greatest liberality granting passes and it is believed captains will not refuse enlisted men passes when they are merited by good conduct at the post."[153] At least one of Bozeman's more enterprising madams would attempt to bypass the restrictions on visiting the town. Private William White noted in his diary that "the French Lady" brought her wagon on the military reservation, undoubtedly against regulations and the commander's wishes, in order to make it easier for soldiers to come "visit" her.[154]

The paymaster records for the frontier army do not survive. However, the amount of money brought into the local economy by the soldiers can be estimated by taking the yearly number of soldiers provided on the post returns and multiplying it by thirteen dollars, the enlisted man's monthly pay, and then multiplying that by twelve months. The estimated amount may not have gone entirely into the Bozeman economy, as some soldiers may have sent money to relatives or purchased goods from the East.

The payroll from Fort Ellis ranged from a high of $70,044 in 1876 to a low of $19,344 in 1881. The Great Sioux War of 1876 brought more soldiers and more money into the area. The perceived and real threat of

Graph with the estimated payroll from enlisted personnel at Fort Ellis from 1867 to 1885. While not all the money would make its way into the Bozeman economy, a large portion of likely would. *By author.*

Indian problems provided a windfall profit for the merchants of Bozeman. When the perceived threat of Indian assaults dropped in the late 1870s and early 1880s, the military moved some troops from Fort Ellis to other posts in more strategic locations. The number of men stationed at the fort sank to an all-time low of 124 in 1881. Through the remainder of the fort's existence, the number of enlisted men held steady at around 150 men, bringing only about a maximum of $23,000 into the local economy annually.

One of the most common items the merchants of Bozeman provided to the soldiers of Fort Ellis was alcohol. Drinking had been a long-term problem for the army but was not a matter exclusively limited to the military. Mining towns, cow towns and seaport towns experienced the problem of large-scale drinking similar to that confronting military towns.[155] Some commanders of Fort Ellis opposed selling their men booze. Captain LaMotte informed the settlers of Bozeman, shortly after construction of the fort began, that selling intoxicating liquor to the soldiers at the fort would be prohibited.

Despite LaMotte's official warning, drinking continued. The 1870 census showed that Bozeman, population ninety-three, had two brewers and three barkeeps. In 1880, the census listed seven brewers, four bartenders and eight saloonkeepers. While the establishment of the breweries and saloons was not solely due to the presence of the fort, their continued success was largely dependent on soldier consumption.

The drinking of the soldiers provided problems at both the fort and in the town. Private William White noted that after a payday, many of his troop

Etching of Bozeman in the early 1870s that first appeared in the *Pacific Rural Press* from San Francisco (1872). The Bridger Mountains in the background are more interpretive than realistic, though the access to Bridger Canyon is visible.

"got up with large felling heads."[156] Soldiers often became so drunk they not only created fights in town but also caused other problems back at the fort. In the early months of 1873, two privates from Company F of the Second Cavalry urinated in the company quarters while intoxicated, and another from Company A of the Seventh Infantry "fouled his bunk and floor" of the company quarters.[157]

Drinking and carousing became problematic for both the fort and the town. Military leaders usually saw drunkenness as a breakdown of military discipline. Garrison court-martial records listed several instances in which men left the post without permission or overstayed passes. For example, on February 19 and 20, 1872, a few days after a payday, eighteen soldiers left the post without permission and became so drunk as to be unfit for duty. Even when ordered to town to retrieve a soldier who was absent without leave (AWOL), Sergeant John Davis decided to join the soldier he was sent to retrieve "at a house of ill repute…and there became so drunk as to be [un]able to perform any military duty." Some commanders of Fort Ellis vainly tried to prevent the settlers from selling their men booze. The post's first commander, Captain Robert S. LaMotte, informed the settlers of Bozeman that selling intoxicating liquor to the soldiers at the fort would be prohibited and later used military force against the civilians of Bozeman when they refused to comply with his directives.[158]

With large numbers of drunken men in town, violence, conflict and mayhem often occurred. There were disturbances among the soldiers themselves, as well as between soldiers and civilians. In 1871, the town authorities tried to send a message to the soldiers at the fort by bringing an infantry sergeant before the justice of the peace for a violent outbreak in a brothel while under the influence of alcohol and possibly laudanum. The editor of the Avant Courier took the opportunity to reinforce the town's position by writing that "we hope this provides a warning to the soldiers from Fort Ellis who visit the city." The "respectable" elements of Bozeman society disapproved of the soldiers' drinking while the saloonkeepers profited from the soldiers' thirst.[159]

Yet, there was opportunity for more than just the barkeeps when soldiers became drunk. Less principled settlers swindled the drunken soldiers out of (or outright stole) their equipment. For example, in 1869, Private Michael Foley left the fort without permission and went to Bozeman and bartered his cavalry great coat, a long, heavy wool overcoat, in exchange for money to purchase alcohol. Private Vickerman either sold, lost or allowed his great coat to be stolen while in a drunken stupor four years later. Private Joseph

Hana became so drunk in 1871 that he allowed his government horse to be stolen. The same thing happened to Private John Irving two years later. However, stealing was not limited to civilians. On December 7, 1870, Private Alfred W. Monday stole a pair of cavalry boots from his company quarters and intended to go to Bozeman to sell or trade them.[160]

The merchants were keenly aware of the importance of the soldiers' pay. With potentially $19,000 to $70,000 dollars coming into the town annually from the army payroll, they had good reason to anticipate the paymaster's arrival. On at least one visit, the newspaper reported that the paymaster disbursed $12,000 in one day.[161] The *Courier* often announced the troops' payday. For example, on May 10, 1877, it reported:

> *Paymaster* [John E.] *Blaine and Mr. Blaine Walker paid off the command on Monday. We wonder whether these gentlemen know how welcome they always are both at Bozeman and the post; and that, too, outside of any business considerations.*[162]

Yet the soldiers did not always spend their pay as the local merchants would have liked. The soldiers were aware of the importance of their pay to the merchants and used their spending power as a voice of protest when they felt they were treated unfairly. One soldier wrote to Bozeman's economic community through the *Courier* in 1880:

> *If Bozeman merchants did not receive the usual patronage of the soldiers, they must let their comparatively high prices for goods account for it. So long as we can buy goods in the east at prices much less than those demanded for them here, and we can get Eastern goods sent to us free of charge, we will forgo your establishments.*[163]

The implied threat did not carry as much impact as it might have ten years earlier. By the early 1880s, the town had undergone a vibrant change that brought it out of the adolescent transition stage into that of a secure community. Its population and economy became more diverse, and the physical character of the town gave an air of permanence as the buildings became better constructed and assumed a more regular order. By the time the Northern Pacific Railroad arrived in 1883, Bozeman's existence was not as fragile as it had been when the fort was established sixteen years earlier.

A clear sign of the town's security was the new diversity of local commerce. A few establishments offered a variety of products and services in the early

An etching of the brick kiln in Bozeman. The increased use of brick for buildings demonstrated both economic development as well as a feeling of security in the stability of the settlement. *From Leeson's* History of Montana *(1885).*

years of the settlement, but businesses had become more specialized by the 1880s. The 1880 census shows that the town had two hotels and two boardinghouses, ten general stores, one milliner, one tailor, two boot shops, two watchmakers, one jeweler, three blacksmiths and wagon shops, one harness maker, two liveries, three carpenters, one gunsmith, two brickyards, two tin shops, one paint shop, one printing firm, one photographer and one bakery in a total population of almost one thousand people. One indication that the town felt greater economic security in its future was the presence of two banks. The soldiers could visit several new saloons in addition to the early establishments of the settlement. The Tivoli, a brick beer hall, offered dancing and food in addition to beer and whiskey. Cy Mount's Saloon specialized in gambling and provided live music by a ladies' orchestra. Sackett's Harbor offered a more dignified saloon that kept disturbances to a minimum.[164]

The fort provided not only dollars for local merchants but also surplus equipment at a somewhat inexpensive price. The quartermaster receipts for

1884, kept by Lieutenant G.C. Doane, list items such as tents, buffalo coats and fur hats as "unserviceable" and "to be sold in local market."[165] After one sale of surplus clothing, the *Courier* reported:

> *Since the Government sale of clothing at Fort Ellis last week, our citizens have been metamorphosed into soldiers—so far as wearing of the blue goes to make-up the soldier. The visitor to Bozeman will also notice that our male population have adapted the use of a new style of hat, which, if they do not present a comely appearance, possess the more desirable merit of being cheap.*[166]

The sale of surplus items also included equipment. The post operated its own sawmill to maintain a steady supply of lumber for the maintenance of the fort. In 1877, the fort purchased a new engine and sold the old one to W.L. Perkins for $255.70. Even still, some civilians did not always wait for the army to sell some items before they took possession. One enterprising citizen stole the bridge that crossed the East Gallatin River by the post. A soldier wrote to the *Courier* and asked with dripping sarcasm, "Who stole the suspension bridge at the first crossing of the creek above the post? This fine U.S. structure has been carried off bodily, but danger to life and limb departed with it."[167] In 1869, three Springfield rifles were discovered missing and reported to be in the hands of miners at Emigrant Gulch, about fifty miles away. Major Brisbin ordered a detail to proceed to the area and retrieve the guns.[168]

The infusion of Fort Ellis's federal dollars came at a time when it was greatly needed by the community of Bozeman. Though the Gallatin Valley was a fertile and productive area, hard times seemed imminent before the establishment of the fort. Agricultural production outpaced demand in the young territory, and prices of staples dropped. The army stopped travel over the Bozeman Trail in the winter of 1867–68. The decrease in this traffic hurt the businesses of Bozeman, which stood as the first sentinel of settlement after six hundred miles of overland travel. The establishment of Fort Ellis helped curb the forces working against the small community by providing a large market for the crops of the valley and a contingent of willing consumers. In the final analysis, according to M.A. Leeson, military posts, especially Fort Ellis, "added greatly to the prosperity of all classes in the area."[169]

The brick buildings, such as the Tivoli, also indicated a greater confidence in the future, prompting merchants to make a greater investment in the

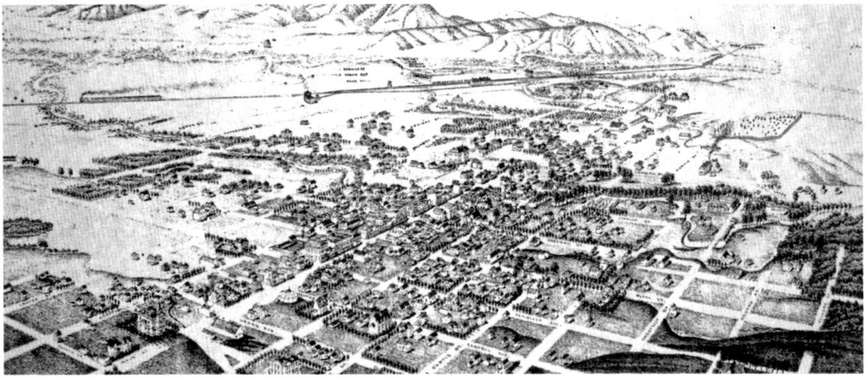

Etching of Bozeman in the early 1880s that appeared in the *Avant Courier*, January 3, 1884. In the decade or so since the previous etching from the early 1870s, the town had undergone significant growth. Note the presence of the Northern Pacific Railroad in the background. The words "Fort Ellis" appear in the background to the right along the tracks, but no buildings are depicted.

community. William Tracy opened a brick works in the mid-1870s, allowing construction of more permanent buildings. The original log buildings gave way to frame structures, and many of those eventually gave way to brick. Streets became more orderly with a more clearly defined business district separated from residential areas. The town gradually evolved into a more stable and permanent community. It was platted in 1878 and became officially incorporated in 1883. Bozeman organized a fire department in 1884. With the growth of stability came a need for more organized schools. Perhaps the greatest indicator of stability and permanence in the young community was the construction of a $14,000 brick school building in 1876–77.[170]

Most of the town had eagerly awaited the coming of the railroad and the access it would provide to eastern markets. The economic importance of the fort began to fade when the trains finally appeared in 1883. The city's future seemed more assured than ever. In addition, the railroad improved the military situation, as troops could be moved quickly and with greater ease in the sparsely populated territory. In 1884, the army scaled back the number of troops at the post, removing regiments one at a time, starting with the Second Cavalry, until the fort was only a shadow of its former self. The town gave the troops a warm send-off, recognizing their economic importance in the past but not indicating fear of the economic ramifications of their departure in the future. The mayor, John V. Bogert, addressed the departing cavalry and crowd, proclaiming of the Second Cavalry: "For many years our social and business intercourse have brought us and them into close relation."[171]

Bogert realized the dynamics of the relationship between the town and the fort. The business relationships brought stability to the area. Despite his appropriately warm words for the occasion, the economic relationship between the fort and town was more complex and included conflict, tension and anxiety. For the community, this tension was both internal and external. The civilians were very conscious of the economic potential of the fort and often perfidiously took advantage of the military dollars, adding to tension between the town and the fort. Bozeman's businessmen acted both honestly and dishonestly to draw hard currency from the federal government into the local economy. Nevertheless, the economic input caused agitation in addition to needed economic stimuli.

4
THE SOCIETIES OF BOZEMAN AND FORT ELLIS

Fort Ellis and Bozeman were separate societies that came into contact because of proximity, economic affiliation and mutual circumstance. Their distinctly different sets of social rules and expectations defined their interactions. The rules of interaction were largely a result of their social composition. Because military regulations strongly discouraged change, the fort's social structure remained constant throughout its history. However, the society of Bozeman changed from the early years of its existence. The town's society developed as the number and type of inhabitants increased. The change in population caused the development of complex social ties, and these new ties brought a social stability that transformed Bozeman from a loose settlement of people to a community.

To understand the relationship between Fort Ellis and Bozeman, it is necessary to examine the social composition of each society. The censuses of 1870 and 1880 provide important statistical information about the age, sex and place of birth for individuals at the post and in town. The censuses have some limitations, however, and are not always exact representations of the social diversity present. For example, in 1870, the monthly post returns show that when the enumerator counted the soldiers at the fort in June, three companies of cavalry were absent; thus, the enumerator did not record around ninety men.[172]

Another problem with the census figures is that they list only place of birth rather than place of last residence Therefore, a person born in a given state or country may not have been raised there and might feel little connection in any way with that region or country. In addition, some people were recorded with no place of birth on the census schedules, further limiting interpretation. That does not mean that the ethnicity and regionalism should be ignored. The problem simply must be recognized when examining the statistics. The exact numbers are not as important as the general patterns the figures reveal.

One of the most significant demographic features of both the fort and the town was that they were predominantly the domains of young males. In 1870, there were only 30 women to 165 men at the fort, and all of the women over the age of seventeen were married. In 1880, the men outnumbered the women by 230 to 32. As in 1870, there were no single women over the age of seventeen. If the soldiers at the post thought of going to Bozeman to find female companionship, they would surely have been disappointed. In 1870, men outnumbered women 69 to 24 with only 3 women listed as single: a twenty-two-year-old teacher, a thirty-three-year-old restaurant owner and a fifty-three-year-old widow.

Age distribution among the men in both the town and at the fort indicates that the greatest number of individuals were between the ages of twenty and forty. In 1870, Fort Ellis listed ninety-eight men (59.30 percent) in their twenties and another thirty-three men (20.01 percent) between the ages of thirty-one and forty. The town of Bozeman had almost an even split in these ranges with twenty-five men (36.23 percent of the town's male population) between the ages of twenty-one and thirty, and twenty-seven men (39.13 percent) between ages thirty-one and forty.

AGE DISTRIBUTION, FORT ELLIS, 1870

	Males		Females	
Age Range	Number	Percent	Number	Percent
<10	10	6.06	9	30.00
11–20*	13	7.87	8	26.66
21–30	98	59.39	8	26.66
31–40	33	20.01	4	13.33
41–50	7	4.21	1	3.33
51–60	4	2.43	0	0.00
61+	0	0.00	0	0.00
Total	165	84.62	30	15.38

* Under the age of seventeen: 10 males and 9 females

AGE DISTRIBUTION, BOZEMAN, 1870

	MALES		FEMALES	
AGE RANGE	NUMBER	PERCENT	NUMBER	PERCENT
<10	6	8.69	7	29.16
11–20*	6	8.69	2	8.33
21–30	25	36.23	10	41.66
31–40	27	39.13	3	12.5
41–50	3	4.34	2	8.33
51–60	2	2.89	0	0.00
61+	0	0.00	0	0.00
Total	69	74.19	24	25.81

* Under the age of seventeen: 8 males and 7 females

Ten years later, in 1880, the town's male population had shifted toward a younger average as the civilians began to have children. Bozeman had 98 male children (17.98 percent of the town's males) under age ten and 55 teenagers (10.09 percent). The fort listed 11 male children under age ten (4.78 percent) and 5 teenagers (2.17 percent). Both the town and the fort showed most of their 1880 male population in the twenty-one- to thirty-year-old range. The fort counted 127 (55.22 percent) men in that range and the town 148 (27.15 percent). The population of Bozeman had a male population of 130 men (23.85 percent) in their thirties while the fort's population of men in their thirties numbered 67 men (29.13 percent). The town also had a much larger population over the age of forty. Bozeman listed 83 men (15.23 percent) in their forties and 22 men (4.04 percent) in their fifties; 6 men (1.100 percent) were in their sixties, and 3 (0.55 percent) were over the age of seventy. The fort listed 19 men (8.26 percent) in their forties and only 1 man (0.43 percent) over the age of fifty.

The 1870 age distributions of the women at the fort and the town reveal similar patterns. The majority of the women at the fort were also under the age of thirty. The census showed that there were nine girls (30.00 percent of all females at the post) under the age of ten, eight (26.66 percent of all females) in their teens and eight in their twenties. Four listed their ages in the thirties (13.33 percent of all females) and one in her forties. The town showed the majority of its females under thirty as well, but with an older average. Seven girls (29.16 percent of all females) in the town were under the age of ten, but there were only two (8.33 percent) female teenagers. Ten women (41.66 percent) were listed in their twenties, three (12.5 percent) in their thirties, two (8.33 percent) in their forties and one (4.2 percent) in her fifties.

AGE DISTRIBUTION, FORT ELLIS, 1880

	Males		Females	
Age Range	Number	Percent	Number	Percent
<10	11	6.06	9	30.00
11–20*	5	7.87	4	26.66
21–30	127	59.39	10	26.66
31–40	67	20.01	7	13.33
41–50	19	4.21	2	3.33
51–60	1	2.43	0	0.00
61+	0	0.00	0	0.00
Total	230	87.77	32	12.23

* Under the age of seventeen: 11 males and 10 females

AGE DISTRIBUTION, BOZEMAN, 1880

	Males		Females	
Age Range	Number	Percent	Number	Percent
<10	98	17.98	86	15.78
11–20*	55	10.09	59	19.22
21–30	148	27.15	61	19.87
31–40	130	23.85	56	18.24
41–50	83	15.23	24	7.82
51–60	22	4.04	15	4.88
61+	9	1.65	6	1.95
Total	545	63.97	307	36.03

* Under the age of seventeen: 121 males and 115 females

The 1880 census indicates that the female population at both the fort and the town became more evenly distributed without a large spike in the twenty-year-old range. The fort recorded nine girls (28.12 percent of the females at the post) under the age of ten and four (12.50 percent) teenagers. Ten women (31.25 percent) were in their twenties, seven (21.87 percent) in their thirties and two (6.25 percent) in their forties. The town had a large increase in the number of female children. There were eighty-six girls (15.78 percent of Bozeman females) listed under the age of ten and fifty-nine (19.22 percent) teenage girls. Sixty-one (19.87 percent) women were in their twenties, fifty-six (18.24 percent) in their thirties and twenty-four (7.82 percent) in their forties. Only fifteen women (4.88 percent) were in their fifties, and four (1.3 percent) were in their sixties. Two women (0.65 percent) were over seventy.

At the fort, the officers tended to be married whereas the enlisted men were much more likely to be single. Of the 12 officers in 1870, 10 (83.3 percent) were married, while only 10 of the 190 enlisted men (5.3 percent) were married. In 1880, the pattern remained similar. Of the 11 officers, 9 (81.8 percent) were married while only 9 of the 181 enlisted men (4.9 percent) were married.

The largest single block of soldiers came from overseas. The 1870 census listed fifty (25.91 percent) of the men at the post as born outside the United States. The largest ethnic group came from Ireland, where nineteen men were born. Germany contributed nine soldiers, and there were eleven Canadian-born soldiers, six British, two Scottish and one each French, Swiss and Russian. In 1880, the census recorded ninety-four (36.15 percent) of the fort as being of foreign birth. Ireland and Germany were still the largest contributors with thirty-four and thirty-two soldiers, respectively. Nine soldiers listed their birthplace as England, two from Scotland and two from France, and seven listed Canada.[173] Russia, Sweden and Indochina accounted for two men each, and Australia, Holland and the West Indies each accounted for one soldier.

The ethnic composition of Bozeman was somewhat diverse as well but not to the extent of Fort Ellis. In 1870, immigrants accounted for 18.29 percent of the town's population. Unlike the immigrant population of Fort Ellis, Bozeman's immigrants were fewer and not dominated by large contingents of Irish and Germans. The census schedules for Bozeman listed only two Irish, two Chinese, two English, two Prussians, two people from Saxony and one person each from Hanover, Bermuda, Poland, France and Wurtemburg. In 1880, the foreign-born citizens constituted 17.67 percent of Bozeman's population. The Irish made up the largest group with twenty-nine people. The Germans and Chinese constituted the next largest blocks of ethnicity with sixteen and twenty-five townsmen each. England was not far behind with thirteen citizens, while Wales, Scotland, Switzerland, Poland, Norway and Belgium each contributed five native sons to Bozeman's population. The town also had four Frenchmen and six Danes.

The presence of significant numbers of immigrants both in Bozeman and at Fort Ellis probably affected the relationships between the two societies. Since almost one in five people in town came from overseas, civilians likely were more tolerant of the immigrants at the fort. Had the town been mostly homogeneous, the citizens might not have been as friendly toward the soldiers from abroad.

The region of the United States from which the largest number of soldiers came was the Mid-Atlantic, totaling 22.80 percent of the fort's population in 1870 (see Origins of Population, 1870 table). Of the forty-four soldiers from the Mid-Atlantic, twenty-four came from New York, and Pennsylvania contributed sixteen men. One soldier listed New Jersey as his place of birth, while three claimed Maryland as theirs. In 1880, the Mid-Atlantic composed 28.07 percent of the fort's population (see Origins of Population, 1880 table). New York and Pennsylvania still dominated the statistics with twenty-four and thirty-five men, respectively. Maryland was the birthplace of eight soldiers; New Jersey and Washington, D.C., were the birthplace of one man each.

In Bozeman, the Mid-Atlantic incorporated 13.41 percent of the population in 1870. Only two states, New York and Pennsylvania, made up this group with eight and two natives, respectively. In 1880, the Mid-Atlantic comprised 15.86 percent of Bozeman's population (see Origins of Population, 1880 table) and was still dominated by New York, with eighty-eight natives, and Pennsylvania, with thirty-two. Maryland and New Jersey each had two natives while Delaware and the District of Columbia had only one each. Surprisingly, 18.65 percent of the soldiers at Fort Ellis in 1870 came from southern states, most of whom had recently been in direct conflict with the army they now served. The largest contingent of southern-born soldiers (seventeen) came from Missouri, followed by Kentucky with ten, Virginia with five and one each from Florida, Georgia, Mississippi and North Carolina. Ten years later, 11.53 percent of the post's soldiers came from southern states. Louisiana was the home of seven soldiers, followed by Kentucky with six. Four soldiers were natives of Missouri, and three listed their birthplaces as Tennessee and Georgia. Texas and Virginia each had two soldiers at the post, and Alabama and South Carolina had only one.

The South formed the third-largest place of birth for Bozeman in 1870, with 18.29 percent. Seven people came from Missouri, three from Virginia, two from Louisiana and one each from Arkansas, Kentucky and Tennessee. By 1880, the South provided the second-largest block of Bozeman citizens, comprising 18.75 percent of the population. The vast majority, eighty-six people, came from Missouri. Virginia came in a distant second with thirteen natives, followed by Kentucky with twelve. Louisiana accounted for four citizens, while Mississippi and Alabama accounted for three. Georgia and Texas added two each, and one person represented each Arkansas and the Indian Territory.

The Midwest accounted for the birthplace of 21.76 percent of the fort's population in 1870. Sixteen soldiers listed their place of birth as Illinois, ten as Indiana and seven as Ohio. Two listed Michigan while Minnesota and

Iowa each had one native son at the post. In 1880, the Midwest made up 10.77 percent of the fort's population, Ohio being the largest contributor with thirteen. Illinois and Indiana followed with five soldiers each. Wisconsin, Iowa and Minnesota all contributed one man.

The Midwest was the origin of the largest percentage of Bozeman citizens in 1870 at 34.15 percent of the total population. The vast majority came from Ohio, accounting for fifteen people, followed by six from Iowa, three from Illinois and another three from Indiana. Michigan had one native in town. In 1880, 19.59 percent of the population originated in the Midwest. Forty-four people listed Ohio as their place of birth while forty listed Illinois. Iowa contributed twenty-six people to Bozeman's population while Michigan contributed fourteen and Indian thirteen. Twelve citizens came from Wisconsin, eight from Minnesota and six from Nebraska.

The New England states accounted for only 3.63 percent of the population at Fort Ellis in 1870 and 10.00 percent in 1880. In 1870, the distribution among states was fairly even, with Maine, New Hampshire and Rhode Island contributing one soldier each and Vermont and Massachusetts two each. In 1880, Massachusetts dominated the New England–born soldiers with seventeen men. Maine and Vermont each had three representatives, and Connecticut, New Hampshire and Rhode Island had one.

In Bozeman, three New England states contributed 6.10 percent of the population in 1870. Two townsmen came from Connecticut, two from Massachusetts and one from Vermont. In 1880, the number of New England states contributing to the town's population increased, but the percentage declined to 5.16 percent. Vermont had fourteen natives in Bozeman, followed by Massachusetts with eleven. Seven people came from Maine, five from Connecticut, three from New Hampshire and one from Rhode Island.

Western states or territories represented 7.25 percent of Fort Ellis's population in 1870 and 3.46 percent in 1880. The 1870 census listed thirteen children born in Montana, with the oldest being just four years old. The 1880 figures recorded six people at the post born in Montana, one in Colorado and one in Wyoming, the oldest being fourteen.

In Bozeman, the West contributed 9.76 percent of the population in 1870 and 22.96 percent in 1880. The 1870 schedules listed 1 person born in Colorado, 5 in Montana and 8 in Wyoming. The eldest of these was only six years of age. In 1880, 156 people had been born in Montana, the eldest being nineteen years of age. California had 11 native-born individuals; Colorado and Utah had 5, Idaho 2 and Wyoming 4. The eldest of these was sixteen years of age.

ORIGINS OF POPULATION, 1870

Region	Bozeman		Fort Ellis	
	People	% Population	People	% Population
South	15	18.29	36	18.65
Mid-Atlantic	11	13.41	44	22.80
New England	5	6.10	7	3.63
Midwest	28	34.15	42	21.76
West	8	9.76	14	7.25
Foreign	29	18.29	50	25.91

ORIGINS OF POPULATION, 1880

Region	Bozeman		Fort Ellis	
	People	% Population	People	% Population
South	156	18.75	30	11.53
Mid-Atlantic	132	15.86	73	28.07
New England	43	5.16	26	10.00
Midwest	163	19.59	28	10.77
West	191	22.96	9	3.46
Foreign	147	17.67	94	36.15

Thus, the demographic composition of both the fort and town showed similarities. Early in their relationship, single white male populations dominated both. Both had diverse ethnic and regional identities with no single group from one area dominating the population. Within ten years, the number of women in the town increased and stabilized the population while the population at the fort remained dominated by the large population of males.

The society at Fort Ellis was segregated along military lines. The army's strict understanding of hierarchy upheld a stem set of customs that defined military discipline. The system governed the relations of the enlisted men and their families with the officers and their families through strict adherence to deference. The officers of a typical fort occupied the top of the social order. Yet in the post–Civil War army, there was a distinction between officers. After the war, many volunteer officers decided to pursue a professional military career and became a vital part of the regular army. In the new frontier atmosphere, officers of volunteer origins mixed equally with those from the United States Military Academy. Fort Ellis was no different

Photo facing north toward the Bridger Mountains of soldiers in dress uniforms on the parade ground of Fort Ellis. *Courtesy of the Gallatin County Historical Society.*

than other frontier posts in this regard. Established only two years after the end of the war, it had a mixture of West Point graduates and volunteer officers. Despite their origins, most of the officers in the regular army were thoroughly professional and maintained the "neo-feudal standards of chivalry" that defined them as middle-class gentlemen.[174]

The records of the officers who served at Fort Ellis are very incomplete. Those who attended West Point have their service records listed in the Registrar of Graduates and Former Cadets of the United States Military Academy. The 1802–1965 registrar shows that several members of the officer corps had careers reflecting the traditions of military excellence. Lieutenant Charles Schofield was the son of the third-highest-ranking officer in the army, General John Schofield. Lieutenant Edward McClernand's first assignment after graduating from West Point was Fort Ellis. He went on to a distinguished career serving in the Spanish-American and First World Wars and then became the military attaché to Japan, retiring as a brigadier general with a Congressional Medal of Honor. Lieutenant Samuel Douglas, a native of Scotland, received his nomination to West Point from Montana and returned to Fort Ellis for his first posting. Later he served as the adjutant general for the Military District of Montana from 1889 to 1892. Charles Francis Roe came to Fort Ellis as a lieutenant in 1870 and retired in 1889 as a

A large group of officers and their presumed families on the porch of officers' quarters at Fort Ellis. The symmetrical wooden building appears to be a combination of clapboard and log construction. The clapboard may have covered a log superstructure. The image does not conform to the supposed plans for officers' quarters shown on page 55. *Courtesy of the Gallatin County Historical Society.*

major general in the New York National Guard.[175] Lovell Hall Jerome, the son of a prominent New York columnist, graduated from the academy and found himself at Fort Ellis in 1870.[176] Fayette Washington Roe (no relation to Charles F. Roe) came from a military family. His father had served as an officer in the Mexican and Civil Wars, and his grandfather had served in the Revolutionary War.[177] Nathaniel Sweitzer, commander of Fort Ellis from 1873 to 1875, had a brevet rank of brigadier general during the Civil War and served as the aide-de-camp to General George McClellan from 1861 to 1863.[178]

Of the sixty-five known officers who served at Fort Ellis between 1867 and 1886, thirteen attended West Point. Like the volunteer officers, the cadets who entered the military had diverse socioeconomic backgrounds.[179] Cadets of upper-middle-class and military families joined cadets from agricultural and lower-middle-class backgrounds at the school. The lower-middle-class families who sent their sons to the academy often saw West Point and the military as opportunities for social advancement.[180]

Antebellum colleges, including West Point, occupied themselves with the development of character and the production of Christian gentlemen. West Point reached the apogee of character building through the most rigorous

Lieutenant Edward Casey, by Frederic Remington, 1890.

discipline.[181] The academy inculcated the values of duty, honor, loyalty and courage through special conduct classes required at every class level. These courses were offered by the Department of Ethics, which was charged with producing Christian soldiers and gentlemen.[182] Even when postwar colleges began to graduate men with more professional business outlooks, West Point remained conservative and held on to the prewar pattern of classical education.[183]

During the early 1870s, the academy faced some instances in which a few cadets broke the code of moral conduct. The corps responded by banishing the violators without contacting school officials.[184] Six cadets who participated in these events (Lovell Hall Jerome, Edward McClernand, Daniel C. Pearson, Charles Schofield, James Allison and Harry Huntington) would later serve at Fort Ellis.

The strong military caste system prevented close contact between officers and enlisted men. Yet warm personal relationships within the bonds of the rigid order did exist.[185] Hardships of field service and off-duty activities could soften the usually austere formalities.[186] Normally, however, the enlisted men carried on their off-duty lives separate from the officers. The strict etiquette that established boundaries between officers and enlisted men remained even after discharge. In 1869, Captain R.S. LaMotte issued a general order stating that recently discharged men staying at the post were still required to salute officers or be thrown off the reservation. He stressed:

> *The officers are just as much entitled to proper respect being paid them as they always were and the soldier after his discharge is none the better citizen that he leaves his politeness and courtesy behind him with his arms and accouterments.*[187]

The distinction between officers and enlisted men was not the only distinction in the service. Enlisted men themselves were not a monolithic group. With between 25 and 36 percent of the post being of foreign birth, the ethnic diversity created a mixing of customs in the society at Fort Ellis. This diverse ethnicity sometimes created problems, and even a given nationality might demonstrate strong ethnic divisions. In 1874, an Irish Protestant soldier attempted to kill another Irish soldier—a Catholic—who was "overbearing and insulting, and has made [the Protestant soldier] the butt of his insolence, which was carried to an intolerable extent."[188] This type of conflict was the exception, and usually soldiers of common nationality had friendly relations. For example, the German soldiers had a "German Social" in 1880 and invited people from town.[189]

The common experience of the men could help blur the lines of ethnic division. On Saint Patrick's Day in 1880, Irish soldiers organized a celebration for which "applications from many other nationalities [were] received daily for the purpose of being converted into Irishmen for the occasion."[190] The fact that men of other nationalities wanted to be "converted into Irishmen for the occasion" suggests an acceptance of the Catholic Irish and their traditions by some of their fellow soldiers.

Some soldiers distinguished themselves from others by joining organizations. Soldiers at the fort established the Lincoln Lodge Number 10 of the Independent Order of the Good Templars, a national temperance society, in 1873.[191] The garrison court-martial orders indicated that many soldiers did not join this temperance society and continued to drink, often heavily. The division showed that some enlisted men espoused the Protestant middle-class values of nineteenth-century America that objected to the consumption of alcohol. Even some Catholic soldiers embraced these same values as they organized their own temperance society called St. Mary's Total Abstinence Society in 1880.[192]

Many enlisted men kept in touch with the greater American society through the post and company libraries. The post had a library that contained about three hundred works. In addition, one company of infantry and one of cavalry organized their own literary clubs that owned eighty volumes of their own and subscribed to twenty periodicals and newspapers.[193] Soldiers also could go to the town for books. Private William White spent three days examining a geography book he got from town.[194]

Outside of the military personnel, the women at the post also became a distinct social group. The wives of the officers held high status in the social relations at the post and changed the tone of society in a regiment.[195] Unlike the enlisted men's wives, whose employment as laundresses made them worthy of legal recognition, the army did not legally recognize officers' wives. Even without formal acknowledgment in military regulations, they held higher social standing in the fort's society than did the enlisted men's wives. The officers' wives at Fort Ellis, as at most other posts in the West, lived in private quarters adjacent to the parade ground with their husbands, reflecting their acknowledged role as part of the regiment. The laundresses, however, occupied quarters separate from their husbands on the periphery of the post, some 250 yards from the parade ground in the case of Fort Ellis.[196]

The officers' wives created a social caste system similar to that of their husbands. A commanding officer's wife headed the hierarchy and was referred to as the K.O.W., as the literal abbreviation had unfavorable implications. The officers' wives used traditional feminine tasks such as cooking, sewing and visiting to pass the time and become very close to one another.[197]

Whether the garrison worked like a "family," as Elizabeth Custer claimed in her book *Boots and Saddles*, depended largely on the personalities of the individual officers and their wives. Occasionally, officers' families were not on speaking terms with one another; at other times, the women were extremely loyal to one another and forged a tightly knit society that did make the regiment a "family."[198] The women at Fort Ellis led this process, in harmony with the nineteenth-century "cult of true womanhood" or "domesticity" that designated women as the guardians of middle-class morals and values.[199] For example, on Christmas Day 1879, the wife of the commanding officer, Lieutenant Colonel Alexander, assumed the

Belle McKeever and Lt. Edgar Wheelock, by Frederic Remington, 1899.

matriarchal position at the fort and gave a Christmas party at her expense and provided presents for all the children.[200]

As guardians of the home, officers' wives brought elements of material culture with them to the isolated posts on the frontier to bring comfort in their squalid conditions.[201] Colonel Albert G. Brackett, a former commander of Fort Ellis, commented that officers' wives usually brought parlor furniture and other valuable but impractical items to the West. Brackett felt that bringing such useless items only induced greater hardship on officers and their wives when moving to and from the posts.[202]

The best direct account of female life at Fort Ellis comes from the letters of Frances Marie Antoinette Mack Roe. As a young girl, she had gone to a private school in Elmira, New York, and could trace her ancestry in America to before the Revolutionary War.[203] Her stay at the fort brought her into contact not only with the officers but also with the enlisted men, who showed her every courtesy. The concept of "true womanhood" compounded by the scarcity of women might have caused the enlisted men to treat her as somewhat of a curiosity. Roe enjoyed the soldiers' thoughtfulness and stated, "Nothing pleases me more than to have the enlisted men pay me some little attention."[204]

The enlisted men offered to help her when the fort was caught in a particularly bad hail storm. In January 1879, Roe's husband brought her with him on a detached duty at the logging camp and sawmill up Bridger Canyon. There Roe ate and socialized with the enlisted men. In turn, the men cooked a special pie for her as well as gave her a pet squirrel to replace one that had recently died.[205]

One common denominator that all the social segments shared was the physical environment of the fort. The fort, located more than five thousand feet above sea level, had rather cool weather year-round. The meteorological reports for 1870–74 showed that the mean temperature for July (the warmest month of the year) ranged from a chilly sixty degrees Fahrenheit in 1872 to seventy degrees in 1874. During the same period, the mean temperature for December (the coldest month of the year) ranged from eleven degrees Fahrenheit in 1873 to twenty-nine degrees in 1870.[206]

The cold weather brought further hardships, for when the East Gallatin River froze in winter, there were no other accommodations for bathing. The buildings at the fort varied in quality and size. The company barracks contained kitchens and mess rooms with stoves for warming. However, there were "no special means of ventilation, the combination of chinks between logs and high winds affording generally more than the requisite amount of air for comfort during nine or ten months of the year." Some of the log barracks were replaced with framed buildings as the older ones deteriorated due to age and weather. Officers lived two families to a building in houses along the south side of the parade ground and near the hospital. Originally, each had four rooms, but additions through the years changed the layout so that some had seven rooms and others five. In 1875, two sets of officers' quarters were framed, and the rest were log buildings. Unlike the enlisted men's barracks, the post surgeon considered the officers' quarters "warm and comfortable."[207]

Towns in the West did not start as communities. Communities are characterized by the interrelations of familiarity that arise out of the personal contact of daily life. Common experience and emotional bonds create a sense of security and stability. Large numbers of single males who had no intention of permanently settling dominated the earliest urban centers of the West. These men generated no explicit ties to a settlement and impeded their development into communities. Instead, these rootless men created anxiety as they took the celebrated frontier individualism to excess in drinking, gambling and violence.[208]

In the early years of Bozeman's existence, both the town and Fort Ellis were dominated by a large population of single males. As the town moved toward economic and social stability, the presence of women became more prominent. In 1870, there were 24 women out of 93 people in the town (26 percent of the population), and women made up 30 out of 195 (15 percent) people at Fort Ellis. When the 1860 census was taken, women accounted for 307 out of the 852 inhabitants (36 percent), or slightly more than one-third of the town's population. In contrast, there were only 32 women out of 230 people at the fort (14 percent). Bozeman's female population doubled between the 1870 and the 1880 censuses while the female population at the fort remained essentially the same.

Nineteenth-century society perceived women as the antidote to the excess of men on the frontier. Men of the nineteenth-century West generally agreed that only respectable middle-class women could create an ordered society since women were regarded as the guardians of the home, as justified by the "cult of true womanhood."[209] Consistent with women's presumed moral superiority, the unrestrained behavior of men on the frontier shocked and alarmed the women who witnessed it. When Mrs. Melinda Rich arrived in Bozeman in 1866 or 1867, she described the character of the town:

> *The sounds of murderous pistol shots were often heard at midnight or in the early morning hours. Then followed the measured tread of men's feet as they bore some dead or wounded body away…The deadly thing that usually instigated the murders and the angry shouts and curses which so often rang out upon the midnight air, was sold in low board houses.*[210]

Fight in the Street, by Frederic Remington, published in *Century Magazine*, October 1888.

Rich attributed the disorderly behavior of the men to the consumption of alcohol that, as a good Presbyterian, she particularly frowned on.

Without women eligible for marriage, early Bozeman's dominant single male population had no need for or intention of creating permanent roots in the town. The uncertainty of the town's future created anxiety, particularly among those who wanted to form an economically stable society, namely the merchants. Businessmen required a secure clientele of permanent residents who propagated and created a continuous, stable and less volatile social system. Consequently, women were viewed as essential to the establishment of stability consistent with their Protestant middle-class values.

The middle-class women the merchants wanted to marry were not available in Bozeman. Some Bozeman businessmen, therefore, went east to find wives and brought them back to the West. William H. Tracy and Lester Willson traveled east in late 1868 and early 1869 to find wives. Tracy returned to Bozeman with his spouse on June 4, 1869, and Willson returned with his wife a week later.

Tracy's newly wedded wife, Sarah, claimed that when she arrived in Bozeman she was "somewhat of an object of curiosity." The absence of women in the area caused her arrival from Ohio to be quite a spectacle, as the townspeople had eagerly awaited her coming. They wanted to see how Mr. Tracy had fared in his search for a female companion, bringing Sarah no lack of attention during her first days in town. At the Guy Hotel, her second dinner in town brought "seventy-five extras for supper," the owner later admitted.[211]

During her first week in town, Sarah Tracy made contacts with Bozeman's female society. She claimed that there were only fourteen women in Bozeman when she arrived in 1869, eight of whom visited her during the first ten days of her arrival and the rest sporadically after that. The townswomen included businessmen's wives like Mrs. Alderson, wife of the first Methodist minister and a town merchant; Mrs. Rich and Mrs. Willson, whose husbands owned Willson and Rich Retail Establishment; Mrs. Guy, whose husband owned and operated the Guy Hotel, and her daughter, Sophia; Mrs. Nobel, wife of a lumber mill owner; the wife of the town's only architect, Mrs. Beall; and Mrs. Story, whose husband had diverse economic interests that included ranching, farming, freighting and a partnership in a store with Mr. Davis.[212]

These women formed their own social circle in town. The Guy Hotel was the center where they gathered most often to socialize. They bonded together and could depend on each other in the small community, such as when Mrs. Story took particular care in helping the young seventeen-year-old Sarah Tracy become accustomed to her new role as a wife. Mrs. Story taught Sarah how to cook and entertain properly.[213]

As the number of "respectable" middle-class women grew in Bozeman, the differentiation among the female inhabitants became even more marked. Prostitution naturally had flourished in towns dominated by a large population of unattached males. In the western settlements, prostitution and brothels became a central feature of town life. With the introduction of "respectable" middle-class women who nurtured and defended the Protestant Christian morals of society, the prostitutes became visible symbols of those who acted outside the boundaries of acceptable feminine society. In addition, prostitutes could be held up as examples to young girls of those who trespassed against the norms of middle-class female behavior.[214] Bozeman had several brothels that employed only Chinese women.[215] Since the Chinese were widely discriminated against, this added further isolation from middle-class society. In western settlements, red-light districts and Chinatowns usually were near each other. Since brothels and prostitutes fulfilled a community's need to relieve unattached men's sexual energy, they were segregated but not banished.

As middle-class couples began to have children, providing those children with proper moral and intellectual training was important to those who desired social stability. The first school in Bozeman opened in 1865, only a year after the founding of the town.[216] The second teacher in Bozeman's school was Miss Florence Royce. She stayed only one year but was the first of many young single women to teach in the town. Between 1865 and 1878, ten of the eighteen teachers in Bozeman were women, eight of whom were unmarried young women.[217]

With women's perceived moral superiority and their natural duty to protect middle-class values, the classroom was a natural extension of the home and therefore the realm of "true womanhood." Spreading correct Protestant morality, particularly to young girls, was so important to some in town that Gertrude Crittenden, the daughter of Reverend L.B. Crittenden, opened the Gallatin County Female Seminary in 1873.[218]

Many young female teachers, such as Miss Florence Royce, taught in town only until they became married. But like others, they gained a certain amount of independence from teaching. Miss Amy Sweet not only taught in the school but also became a clerk in the post office.[219] The West offered women opportunities in business, and at the same time, they could remain part of the female sphere of domesticity. The 1870 census of Bozeman showed that one independent woman owned a restaurant, and the 1880 census listed three women who owned boardinghouses.

As the town became more stable, the schools became better organized and hired more teachers. By 1878, the public schools in Bozeman employed four teachers (three of whom were women) and one principal and had separate high school and elementary programs. Perhaps the greatest indicator of stability and permanence in the young community was the construction of a brick school building in 1876–77.[220]

Like schools, churches emerged as extensions of the female sphere in young western towns and became leading institutions for shaping morals. Because of the early arrival of William W. Alderson, a Methodist minister from Illinois, the Methodist church was the first church to build a separate building in 1866.[221] Women took a very active role in the church affairs. Sarah Tracy organized the Sunday school. The Ladies' Aid Society took the lead in raising funds through a subscription to build a more permanent brick church and parsonage. When the Presbyterian church formally organized in 1872, six of the nine communicants were women.[222]

Early churches in Bozeman, from Leeson's *History of Montana* (1885). Note the progress from the small log structure that served as Bozeman's first church.

Despite early domination by a particular church, settlements in the West showed a Protestant unity that was not as common in other parts of the country.[223] The Methodists in Bozeman allowed other denominations the use of their building until the Presbyterians and Episcopalians could erect their own churches. When Bishop Tuttle of the Episcopal church came to

Bozeman on his rounds through Montana, Mrs. Willson and Mrs. Rich always offered substantial help in organizing services and providing him a place to stay, even though they were both Presbyterians.[224]

The churches created social ties within the town beyond the realm of work. They united members of the community with similar social concerns and interests. The evangelical Protestant denominations shared a common outlook against alcohol consumption and other behaviors that contradicted middle-class values. Members of the different congregations could unite their efforts through organizations such as temperance lodges. Bozeman had three different temperance lodges to encourage abstinence.[225]

The organizations often accepted members from both sexes and all classes. Members could gather and create contacts that would develop into intimate social relations.[226] As these networks grew, the settlement of Bozeman moved further toward becoming a community. Temperance lodges were only one type of the many lodges that were organized in Bozeman. The people in town established other fraternal lodges such as Masonic and Odd Fellow Lodges. The Self-Improvement Society was organized in 1877 "for the purpose of training the moral and intellectual faculties of its members." In addition, some townsmen established the Young Men's Library Association that created Bozeman's first library in 1872. The next year, the Young Men's Christian Association started its own library in the basement of the Methodist Church. Other organizations were based around business ties. Those who sought membership in the Bozeman Grange or the Stockgrowers Association of Gallatin County were pursuing individual interests. However, their pursuit of business contacts or group economic support also brought the people in the community in contact with each other in a social environment.[227]

Political parties and connections were other voluntary associations that members of the community joined. The strong southern influence joined the strong immigrant influence and made Bozeman a Democratic bulwark. As a territory, Montana had strong Democratic sympathies. When Sidney Edgerton, a Republican-appointed governor of the territory, required the first legislature to swear an "iron clad" oath to the Union in 1864, some Democrats with strong Southern sympathies became infuriated. One even chose to resign his seat rather than commit perjury.[228]

In the early years of Bozeman, the Democratic influence became apparent. From 1865 until 1880, Bozeman voted for a Democratic nonvoting territorial delegate to the United States Congress and Democratic candidates for the territorial legislature. Despite the strong

Photo of the rough-hewn log house of William W. Alderson in about 1870. The structure was built in 1865–66 and is representative of the first structures built in Bozeman. As the town grew and developed, the architecture became less vernacular and more refined, using milled lumber or brick; often more ornate; and built according to specific plans. *Courtesy of Renne Library Special Collections, Montana State University, Bozeman, Montana.*

Residence of Lester Willson, purportedly the first house built in Bozeman. *From Leeson's* History of Montana *(1885).*

Democratic influence, there were political divisions. After a local election, John V. Bogert commented in the *Avant Courier*, "A portion of the community has ever been somewhat impulsively progressive, while another portion has been extremely conservative.[229]

The divisions within the community also could be seen in the style and size of the houses people lived in. A guide published in 1883, when the Northern Pacific Railroad arrived, described some of the finer homes in town. On Church Street, the guide described seven "fine brick dwellings" inhabited by, among others, the bank president, Lewis Morril; town founders Daniel E. Rouse and William H. Babcock; and the alderman of the fourth ward, William F. Davis. At the end of the street was the "Castle," occupied by the contractor, merchant and eventually the town's first mayor, J.V. Bogert. The guide claimed, "'The Castle' is as elaborately furnished" on the inside as the outside.[230] The house was later sold to William Babcock.

A settlement in the West did not necessarily constitute a community. A community contained intimate, familiar and stable social ties generated by

The diversity of houses in Bozeman, from Leeson's *History of Montana* (1885). Note the "Castle" of which the town was particularly proud, having noted it in booster literature.

common circumstances and daily personal contact. Bozeman developed from a settlement of loosely associated young men into a community with intimate social and personal ties during the late 1860s and early 1870s. In its early history, the town was dominated by a large rootless population of single men. As more women settled in the town, society became more stabilized since family bonds strengthened the society of the town, thus creating a community.

Fort Ellis, on the other hand, had the elements for a community. Soldiers had daily contact with one another and developed warm friendship that often transcended ethnic lines. The bonds between soldiers likely existed before they even came to the fort as the companies had lived together at other posts. The traditional military social system brought stability to the relationships between different classes of people. And whereas the unattached population of early Bozeman could leave town at almost any time it wanted, the soldiers (not counting deserters) were tied to the area by their assignment. The difference between the fort and town societies was the change that developed over time in their internal interaction. Because the traditional military system obstructed change, the society of the fort remained constant. The caste system in place when Fort Ellis was founded in 1867 was the same as when it closed in 1886. Bozeman, however, had developed from a society of transient males in the late 1860s to an actual community of families with lasting social ties by the mid-1880s.

5
SOCIAL RELATIONS BETWEEN THE FORT AND TOWN

Everything was done with the greatest propriety.

In 1873, a crowd destroyed the log jail in Bozeman. The mob took the inhabitants—a white drifter and an African American who had financial interests in some of Bozeman's brothels—to a slaughterhouse, where the mob hanged the men on the beef-dressing rack. The mob was reportedly drunk, violent and, in the opinion of Judge Langhorne, beyond the ability of the town's sheriff to control. The judge sent a message to Fort Ellis's commanding officer, Colonel Hancock, requesting military aid to prevent the spread of the violence. Hancock led a detachment of cavalry to town, "where…the officers and commander of the post rendered every available means to vindicate supremacy of the law, the preservation of peace, and the maintenance of public order."[231]

The judge's plea for aid from the fort was an attempt to create order from chaos. The middle-class leadership of Bozeman, needing to create a stable atmosphere in the town, called on the military, which also wanted to prevent violent outbreaks in the area. Without order and civility, the middle class would lose its precious base since "respectable" families might leave if they did not feel safe. The need to create "public order" was an essential ingredient for building a community. The economic relations forged between the soldiers at Fort Ellis and the citizens of Bozeman brought the two societies into contact. The economic connections quickly laid the foundation for the social relations, both friendly and unfriendly. When soldiers came to town to drink, disturbances often followed. However, settlers in town endured the commotion as they competed for the soldiers' coveted money. At other times, activities such as sports, theater productions, courting and dances suggested more amicable associations that fostered warm personal friendships.

As dramatic and exceptional as the police action of 1873 was, the fort contributed to the creation of a community in Bozeman in other ways. The fort used its manpower for the building or maintenance of the area when called on by the leadership of the town. In addition, certain organizations and activities that the fort initiated aided in creating a vibrant social atmosphere that mimicked elements of eastern society. Through these activities, the military aided in forming and strengthening the growing community of Bozeman.

Social relations, however, were largely determined by social status. The officers fraternized with the elite from Bozeman. The enlisted men who joined temperance lodges and aspired to middle-class status associated with civilians who yearned for similar status. This had distinct effects on the relations between the soldiers and the women of the town. The soldiers who chose not to participate in such organizations had a more difficult time interacting with "respectable" women in a town where the ratio of men to women was so high.

As divisive as the social relations sometimes were, the military and civilian communities frequently united in common efforts. The fort aided Bozeman in becoming a less violent and more stable settlement. Through cooperation, Fort Ellis and Bozeman supported each other in their existence on the frontier.

In the nineteenth century, middle-class America saw drinking as a major moral concern. To fight the problem, middle-class Protestants started a temperance movement that combined both secular and religious approaches to self-discipline. The goals of the temperance movement were novel solutions to the problems created by a growing industrial working class that sought relief from the pressures of factory work through excessive drinking.[232]

Protestant, middle-class, evangelical elements of Methodist, Baptist, Congregationalist and Presbyterian churches directly shaped the movement's progress. The middle-class culture and all who aspired to middle-class status were the most deeply influenced by the temperance ethic. Temperance and sobriety were characteristics that distinguished an individual with the desired status of middle-class morals.[233]

Soldiers of all generations have had a long history of drinking. Since garrison duty on the frontier proved to be very lonely and tedious, soldiers

The Mill and the Still, a temperance political cartoon from *Harper's Weekly*, August 18, 1883. The temperance movement attempted to tie prosperity and middle-class values to the limited consumption of alcohol.

were more inclined than ever to drink, and the saloons in Bozeman became a magnet for the drinking soldiers at Fort Ellis.[234]

With large numbers of drunken men in town, violence, conflict and mayhem often occurred. These problems divided both the fort and town communities. The "respectable" elements of Bozeman society disapproved of the soldiers' drinking, while the saloonkeepers profited from the soldiers' thirst. At the post, the commanding officers saw drinking break down military discipline and efficiency. The town and the fort blamed each other for the problem. However, despite the divisions that drinking created, the efforts to combat the problem through temperance societies brought elements from both communities together.

The army's enlisted men generally fell outside the middle-class status. The post–Civil War army attracted a good number of petty criminals, shady characters and men with legal troubles.[235] At Fort Ellis, a correspondent for *Harper's Magazine* asked why some accomplished theater actors from the East found their way into the garrison. The commanding officer replied that "trouble and more often drink, drove them into the army."[236]

It was the social characteristics of the fort's population that the middle class associated with the perception of heavy drinkers. The large immigrant population, particularly the German and Irish Catholics, were perceived by middle-class Protestants as impeding their work against alcohol. To a certain extent, alcohol consumption did exist within a cultural context, as much as food or clothing. For example, citizens of the United Kingdom (including Ireland) and Germany, two nationalities well represented at the fort, consumed twice as much alcohol per capita as "Americans."[237]

In addition to nationality, the population of Fort Ellis, as well as some elements of Bozeman, belonged to social categories perceived as most likely to drink heavily. According to the literature of the time, the West and its rootless population of young males fit into most of the conventional models of a nineteenth-century heavy drinker as younger, lower-class, unskilled and highly mobile men.[238]

The saloonkeepers of Bozeman joyfully capitalized on these factors and the tradition of military drinking. The cash spent by soldiers aided the retailers, who often struggled economically, especially during the panic of the early 1870s. The flow of cash, judging by the stream of soldiers going to town, was not insignificant. The garrison court-martial records listed several instances where men left the post without permission or overstayed passes. For example, on February 19 and 20, 1872, a few days after a payday, eighteen soldiers left the post "without permission and became so drunk as to be unfit for duty."[239]

Sometimes soldiers just left their official duties and went to town. In 1872, the post herder left the fort's stock unattended and went to Bozeman.[240] Those with official business in town, such as picking up the post's mail, might also stay and visit the saloons.[241] Even when ordered to town to retrieve a private who was absent without leave (AWOL), Sergeant John Davis decided to join that private at a "house of ill-repute…and there became so drunk as to be unable to perform any military duty."[242]

With so many drunken soldiers in town, fights and violence would frequently break out. Disturbances occurred among the soldiers themselves as well as between soldiers and civilians.[243] Confrontation between military personnel and civilians put the soldiers at a legal disadvantage since civil authorities forced "the rule of the road" on the troopers—that is, they were not allowed to defend themselves unless attacked first.[244] Nevertheless, conflicts between civilians and soldiers did exist. In 1871, town authorities brought an infantry sergeant before the justice of the peace, who fined and jailed him for ransacking a brothel while intoxicated by alcohol and benzine.

The editor of the *Bozeman Avant Courier* took this opportunity to voice displeasure with the soldiers' behavior. He wrote, "We hope this provides

A Beautiful Fight Ensued, from Frederic Remington's short story "The Honor of the Troop," published in *Harper's News Monthly Magazine*, June 1899. Soldiers in general were notorious for bad behavior while drinking, and the court-martial records and the *Avant Courier* files indicate Fort Ellis was no exception.

a warning to the soldiers from Fort Ellis who visit." The commanders at the fort were not always sympathetic to the civilians' predicament with regard to the soldiers' drinking. The civilians, after all, supplied the alcohol. The fort's first commander, Captain Robert S. LaMotte, himself an uncompromising total abstainer, decided to take action against certain civilians in town to combat the drinking problem. LaMotte warned the town's citizens that they were not to sell liquor to the soldiers under his command. However, the citizens did not heed his warnings. In 1867, only months after he established the fort, Captain LaMotte declared his own war on the saloonkeepers of Bozeman.[245]

While the consumption of alcohol divided the communities of Bozeman and Fort Ellis, one of the means used to combat the problem united the townspeople and soldiers. The post commanders and the middle-class citizens both encouraged and organized temperance societies in the town and at the fort. Within the temperance movement, there were many organizations. Until the Civil War, the strongest of these was the American Temperance Union. During the war, the financial base and membership of the union began to erode, and by 1865, the remaining members had merged with other organizations.[246] After the war, the center of the movement shifted to the Independent Order of the Good Templars. The Good Templars were organized in Saratoga, New York, in 1851 and, by 1867, had a membership of a half million, as well as far greater influence than any of the organizations that had preceded them. Although the Good Templars denounced alcohol as a source of social evil, they fought it cheerfully through bands, picnics, dances and debates.[247] Unlike their eastern counterparts, western temperance societies did not take their crusade directly against the drinkers but directed their assaults against the sources of drinking—namely, the saloons. They saw the saloon as the mother and symbol of all frontier vices: drinking, gambling, prostitution and violence.[248]

The middle class perceived the Templar societies as a good means by which to combat these problems and to show public adherence to the temperance ethic. Bozeman citizens established three Templar lodges in the late 1860s and early 1870s: the Valley Gem Lodge No. 8, the Fairview Lodge No. 21, and the Fountain Hope Lodge No. 24. Fort Ellis established its own lodge in 1871 as well, named Lincoln Lodge No. 40.[249] Even though the fort and town had separate lodges, a certain amount of crossover occurred. In 1876, William White, a private in the Second Cavalry, applied for membership in the town's Fountain Hope Lodge in addition to his membership at the fort's Lincoln Lodge.[250] Besides the Good Templar lodge, soldiers also established another temperance group called the Sons of Jonadab in 1877, and some Catholic soldiers organized an association known as Saint Mary's Total Abstinence Society in 1880.[251]

The organization of Catholic soldiers into a temperance society indicates a division among the Catholic soldiers at the post. Traditionally, middle-class Protestants viewed Catholics as opponents of the temperance movement. Many of the Catholic soldiers at Fort Ellis probably were no different, and a group of Catholic abstainers shows a marked division within the ranks of the Irish and German Catholic soldiers.

Catholicism had a strong influence in Montana.[252] Catholic missions were established for Plateau Indians dating from 1837 but had less influence in the mining camps than the Protestant denominations.[253] However, strong pockets of Catholic influence developed in the territory, as in Virginia City, where Mass was first said in 1863. Largely due to the efforts of Father Francis DeSmet, a longtime Indian missionary, Helena received a Sisters of Charity convent in 1865, a boarding school for girls named Saint Vincent's Academy in 1869 and Saint John's Hospital and Saint Jerome's Orphan

Home in 1870.[254] Soldiers at the fort, presumably Catholic, had donated to these organizations as early as 1878, when the Sisters of Charity wrote to express their thanks for the contributions to their cause.[255]

The Catholic abstainers at the fort embraced the middle-class values usually associated with the evangelical Protestant denominations. Since sobriety and temperance were symbolic of middle-class respectability in nineteenth-century America, joining a temperance society indicated the social status to which a person aspired. Seeking acceptance through imitation, the Catholic soldiers in the abstinence society sought the prestige given by the middle class and acceptance into that social rank.[256]

Those who joined the Catholic temperance movements wanted to show Protestants that Catholics did have a high sense of civic morality by discouraging one of the most disruptive social behaviors. However, the fact that the fort's Catholic abstainers did not join the Templars or the other temperance groups indicates that the Catholics wanted to maintain their religious identity. The separate Catholic societies came out of their own tradition and usually remained aloof from the Protestant crusade.[257] The soldiers in Saint Mary's Total Abstinence Society at Fort Ellis showed their

Pleading with a Saloon Keeper, by C.S. Reinhart, published in *Harper's Weekly*, March 14, 1874.

continued loyalty to the church by giving the surplus in their treasury to local Catholic charities every year.[258]

Even though they remained separate, the Catholic abstinence society relied on the aid of the Good Templars at the fort, particularly for accommodations. Saint Mary's Total Abstinence Society began to meet in the Good Templars' Hall at the fort very soon after its creation.[259] Similar cooperation existed among all the societies in the area as well. On President Lincoln's birthday in 1880, the temperance societies of the Gallatin Valley "celebrated that event by an elegant supper…provided by Sister and Brother Fredrick, to whom great praise is due for the handsome manner in which they supplied the wants of the inner man. The evening was enlivened by a dramatic and variety entertainment, consisting of a farce, comic sketches, songs, dances, &c."[260]

The six temperance lodges frequently interacted with one another. The fort's Lodge of the Good Templars invited members from town to join its members in a debating society. Speakers, such as the Methodist minister T.C. Iliff, frequently spoke at the fort lodge meetings. The lodge's leaders issued regular invitations through the newspaper to "the brothers and sisters of other lodges" to attend all such meetings. Even people from as far away as Butte came to the fort's lodge meetings.[261] The Templars had a strong enough presence that on an 1884 engraving of a city street, now known as South Tracy Avenue, was the name "Templar Ave," where Mr. Samuel Lewis owned at least one building.

The Templars' activities that organized gatherings and socialization provided a substitute for the saloon. For soldiers in particular, the Templar Lodge provided a dry "clubhouse" where they could unwind separated from the soldiers who drank heavily. Still, though the Templars viewed alcohol as a moral vice, temperance would only be one in a series of necessary reforms that would help create a progressive, prosperous, modern America.[262]

In a town where men outnumbered women three to one and where the ratio of men to "respectable" women was even higher, the class system of the military intensified segregation in those relations between soldiers and civilians. Perceived as more respectable because of their position at the fort, officers were embraced by the middle class of the town socially. The enlisted men who aspired to middle-class status by joining such groups as the Templars could associate with the townsmen who likewise aspired to the same status. The soldiers who did not aspire to the middle-class values did not have as great an opportunity to associate with the middle-class or aspiring middle-class civilians in a social setting.

Images of some properties owned by Samuel Lewis. Note that one building is on "Templar Ave," indicating the strength of the temperance movement in the young town. Templar Avenue is now South Tracy Avenue. *From Leeson's* History of Montana *(1885).*

The fraternal organizations that the officers joined were different from those in which enlisted men enrolled. Though encouraged by commanding officers, the Good Templars appeared to be the domain of the enlisted men since it was they whom the newspaper listed as the elected officials of the club. However, the town had other fraternal societies that the officers and their wives joined. When Lieutenant Grogan donated an engraving to the Young Men's Association, the *Courier* claimed, "The officers and ladies of Fort Ellis have ably assisted this association and several officers are active members."[263] The claim that only officers and their wives took an interest in the organization suggests that enlisted men did not join or participate.

At these clubs the officers and civilians formed social ties. The relationships between certain families in town and the officers' families were close enough for the newspaper to keep people in town abreast of the sickness of Captain Marshall's wife in 1877. In the spring, Mrs. Marshall took seriously ill and was bedridden for several weeks. At one point, a doctor came from out

Frances Marie Antoinette Mack Roe wearing her husband's cadet coatee and her dog Hal. Roe described in vivid detail her experiences at posts in the West, including Fort Ellis. *From* Army Letters from an Officer's Wife *(1909).*

of town for consultation. Weekly announcements kept the people in town posted on her recovery.[264]

In addition, the *Courier* kept the town informed of the departures of the officers and their families. For example, when Lieutenant George Wright was promoted in 1873 and reassigned to Fort Shaw, the *Courier* claimed that he would be missed and that the ladies would "regret the loss of Mrs. Wright from their social circles."[265]

When families prepared to depart the fort for new assignments, citizens from town might attend warm send-offs for their friends. In 1880, when Lieutenant Fayette W. Roe and his wife prepared to leave Fort Ellis, the commanding officer's wife planned a grand surprise party for them. According to the *Courier*, "Quite a large number of young persons went up from town."[266] Mrs. Roe claimed that a band from Bozeman also came and provided enjoyable music. She appreciated her many friends coming out to the fort and giving life to the party and ensuing dance, particularly in "a place where partners are limited."[267] According to the newspaper, the Roes had "made a large circle of warm friends who regret the necessity which suggests the word 'adieu.'"[268] Even after their departure, the officers often kept in touch with the citizens of Bozeman.

The town appreciated the courtesy when former officers came back to visit. Colonel Eugene Baker, for example, visited the town in 1878, and the *Courier* stated, "We wonder who had received the more gratification from the visit, Colonel Baker or the Gallatin Valley."[269] In 1885, Major D.S. Gordon wrote from the presidio of San Francisco to his friends in Bozeman. The *Courier* conveyed his regards "and kind remembrances to numerous acquaintances in the country."[270] Local citizens who traveled east could also relay the good wishes of former officers at the post. William Alderson visited St. Louis in 1877 and reported on his meeting with two former officers of Fort Ellis in the Bozeman newspaper. He claimed that Lieutenants McClernand and McAdams "seemed glad to see me" and asked about friends and matters in Bozeman. Mr. Alderson added that Lieutenant McAdams was particularly interested in certain "Montana belles."[271] Since the officers associated more closely with the middle class, the "Montana belles" in whom Lieutenant McAdams expressed an interest were likely from the "respectable" social set in town.

Together, the "respectable" elements of Bozeman and the officers also enjoyed the opportunities that the local environment provides, such as hunting and fishing. Wives frequently enjoyed these typically masculine activities with their husbands as well.[272] In 1873, Lieutenants Doane and

Coolidge went on a buffalo hunt with their wives accompanied by their friends from town. However, a town physician and member of the party, Dr. Glasher, severely injured himself and cut the trip short.[273]

Dancing was very important as a form of amusement and socialization in the army, and officers sometimes held dances with their social equals from town. Because of the traditions of the military, the officers' dances "provided social occasions which were considerably more elaborate than the size and location of the town merited."[274] The town's middle-class social set also organized its own dances and invited the officers and their wives. Mrs. Roe claimed in 1884 that she and her husband:

> *Attended a pretty cotillion in Bozeman last evening and remained overnight at the hotel...It was quite a large and elaborate affair, and there were present "the butcher, the baker, and the candlestick maker"...* [E]*verything was conducted with the greatest propriety.*[275]

She went on to reveal that there were "five or six fine families in the small place—people of culture and refinement from the East" with whom she and her husband presumably associated. She credited these families with the "building up of the town."[276]

While the officers associated with the town's elite middle class, the enlisted men who joined the Templar lodges associated with the middle class or those who at least aspired to middle-class status. While not necessarily on the same social level with the elite families, those who joined the temperance societies wished for the status given by the middle class and acceptance into the "respectable" set.

The Good Templars' activities provided a valuable opportunity for the enlisted men to socialize with more "respectable" townsmen and women. Where women were so scarce, those women who joined the Templars tended to be those who also embraced middle-class Protestant values. Other women, such as prostitutes, domestic servants or dance-hall girls, and with whom the enlisted men were more apt to come into contact, usually were not members of a Templar lodge.

Dancing constituted one of the most common forms of interaction between men and women, and the Templars' dances often were accompanied by large dinners or comic sketches. The local newspaper reported that at one occasion in 1878, "the dance was well managed. The managing committee and most of the guests being Good Templars, no intoxicating liquors were drank, and the best of order obtained throughout the entire evening."[277]

The civilians enjoyed the soldiers' dances, and the fort's Templars enjoyed the positive reaction from the citizens of Bozeman. One correspondent from the fort reported, "It is gratifying to the managers of the whole affair to hear from invited guests of Bozeman and vicinity that they never enjoyed a more pleasant evening than the one passed here among us." He added that due to the success of the dance, "these social hops will be repeated monthly."[278]

As successful as the Templars' dances were, other groups at the post often failed when they tried to organize their own dances. The Dance Society at the fort attempted to organize a dance in 1876 that was less than a success. They sent an ambulance to town for conveying ladies to the post, but William White claimed that "they was [sic] disappointed to see that none came."[279] The Templars' dances assured a greater guarantee of safety for young "respectable" women than dances organized by ordinary soldiers. Therefore, Templar dances provided greater possibilities for interaction between the sexes.

Even dances given by a specific company added more protection for "respectable" women than those of the enlisted men, since officers attended for part or all of the evening and ensured a measure of order. The company's commanding officer often helped organize and carry out the affairs that also were attended by the citizens of Bozeman. For example, the Third Infantry's Company E held a ball in 1880 at which "several persons from Bozeman were in attendance." The company's officer was in attendance, as the *Courier* reporter wished to express a special "thanks to Captain Mitchell and others for many courtesies shown during the evening."[280] The commanding officer and officers from other units usually made appearances at company balls but only as a matter of ceremony. They danced a couple of dances, including the Grand March, and then retired after a half to three-quarters of an hour. Dancing between soldiers and officers' wives or daughters, as well as between officers and the wives of enlisted men, was strictly against etiquette and could result in a severe reprimand.[281]

Since the enlisted men who were not Templars had fewer opportunities to associate with "respectable" women, their associations centered on the lower-class women, namely prostitutes, dance-hall girls and servants. With a population of men that outnumbered women more than three to one, prostitutes claimed much of the common enlisted men's attention. Soldiers have traditionally been among the most loyal patrons of prostitutes, and most military towns usually had multiple houses for the soldiers' needs. The soldiers at Fort Ellis engaged in significant amounts of sexual activity with prostitutes in town. Between 1870 and 1874, the fort had thirty-nine cases of syphilis and twenty-eight cases of gonorrhea.[282] With sex stripped of affection, the prostitutes only shared a mutual distrust with their customers and gained no real or lasting ties with their "johns," particularly the women who specialized in soldiers. The low pay of the soldiers relegated them to purchasing the services of the old and worn women of a house. Some claimed that when a prostitute "went to the dogs, she went to the soldiers, the lowest level in the customer's scale."[283]

Photo of Lieutenant Gustavus Cheney Doane of the Second U.S. Cavalry was stationed at Fort Ellis. Doane fought in the Civil War as a member of the Second Massachusetts Cavalry. He retired briefly to civilian life after the war but soon returned to military service. In 1870, Doane was the leader of the military escort for the Washburn survey of what would become Yellowstone National Park. The survey became known as the Washburn-Doane Expedition. Doane would later become a member of the Howgate Arctic Expedition to the North Pole in 1880. Doane divorced his first wife in 1878 while at Fort Ellis and married the daughter of Dr. A.J. Hunter two months later. *Courtesy of the National Park Service Archive.*

The prostitute's life was so lonely that more prostitutes retired from the profession by suicide than by accumulating enough wealth or through marriage. The lack of women in the area did not mean absence of flirtation between enlisted men and local girls that might lead to courtship and marriage. Still, since neither the enlisted men nor most of the women ranked high on the social scale, their weddings did not attract more than a brief mention in the newspaper. According to the newspaper, as many as six enlisted men married local girls during the life of the fort. At least one soldier went AWOL to get married, and another was put in jail for drunken and disorderly behavior after his wedding.[284]

In contrast, the single officers at the fort had a greater choice of "respectable" women in town when courting. Two officers married local women, both from the "respectable" class. In 1874, the *Courier* reported the marriage of Lieutenant Charles Roe and the daughter of the merchant and future mayor John V. Bogert.[285] In 1878, Lieutenant Gustavus

C. Doane wed Mary Lee Hunter, daughter of Dr. A.J. Hunter, owner and proprietor of a health spa in the Yellowstone Valley, only three months after his divorce from his first wife, Amelia Link, after rumors of her infidelity.[286] Yet Doane likely had only enjoyed a passing familiarity with Mary Hunter since she lived at St. Vincent's boarding school in Helena. The marriage between the thirty-nine-year-old officer and the nineteen-year-old likely was arranged and suggested a strong association between the officers and the middle class.

The army in Montana improved the infrastructure as much out of military need as an aid to the civilians. The "boosters" of the town benefitted from this as an added advantage to the area that would attract new business and settlers. The soldiers constructed and maintained telegraphic lines and surveyed, constructed and maintained roads.[287] When the road over the Bozeman Pass became impassible, the commander of the post offered the assistance of 150 men and any tools or equipment required to grade the road.[288] Some soldiers, after their enlistment expired, added to the population of the community. When 2 soldiers ended their military career in 1880, they stayed on in Bozeman and built the city's first cheese factory.[289]

Beyond just helping to develop the infrastructure and to boost economic activity, some of the soldiers' leisure pastimes provided Bozeman with entertainments that small towns did not generally experience. To break the monotony of garrison life, some soldiers organized the "Fort Ellis Dramatic and Variety Troupe." The troupe staged elaborate productions not usually found on the frontier. Helena and Virginia City, towns of over 1,000 people in 1870 and 1,500 in 1880, were the only other towns in the Montana Territory to have their own theaters. Bozeman, with fewer than 100 people in 1870 and just fewer than 900 in 1880, did not have a sufficient population to produce an economically viable theater without the time and effort of the soldiers.[290]

The quality of the productions was judged as ranging from very good to average. A correspondent for *Harper's Magazine* commented that the Fort Ellis theater troupe had many performers who "were very good and had played engagements in former years at the best theaters in the east."[291] At times, however, the productions did not live up to the usual standards, and the citizens of Bozeman proved to be a discriminating audience. When attendance dropped due to below-average productions, the soldiers assured the citizens of the town that they were "fixing the problem and hope to see Bozeman well represented" at the future productions.[292] Poor performances were not the only factor limiting town attendance. Bad weather prevented many from going to performances in 1873, and the editor of the *Courier* suggested:

> *To the management, the erection of a horse shed near the theater for the accommodation of town teams. At present, the absence of such a convenience doubtless keeps many from the performances who otherwise would regularly attend.*[293]

The troupe accommodated the civilians by performing productions in town about once a month during the winter. Chestnut Hall and the Young Man's Association Hall hosted the theatricals. The *Courier* reviewer commented that citizens thoroughly enjoyed the performances, and "the frequent and continued applause of the audience evinced the highest appreciation of the efforts of the company." The theater company's trips to town were so well enjoyed that the editors hoped "to have another entertainment in Bozeman before a great while."[294] Because of the favorable reviews given by the *Courier* correspondent Thomas Baker, the actors gave him an honorable membership in the troupe.[295]

The citizens of town enjoyed the fort's theater enough that, when the theater building at the post burned down in 1872, they came to the troupe's aid in building a new one. In the same article in which the *Courier* reported the destruction of the building, the manager of the theater troupe appealed to the citizens of Bozeman to donate money "for the purpose of speedily constructing a new theater building." The editor of the newspaper added, "We trust that everyone will respond and reward this indefatigable manager to such an extent that this place of amusement may soon have its door open."[296] Four months later, after the contributions of townsmen, the theater reopened with a stage sixty-five feet wide by thirty-eight feet deep and with a seating capacity for about two hundred people.[297]

In the summer, the citizens of town and the soldiers engaged in frequent baseball games. Baseball had become a craze enjoyed by all classes in mid-nineteenth-century American society. John Montgomery Ward, a star professional player in the 1870s, claimed that "the game is suited to the national temperament. It requires strength, courage, and skill; it is full of dash and excitement."[298]

Sports teams unified small settlements, both civilian and military, and served as a source of community pride. Just as now, in small towns and garrisons everybody presumably knew someone on the community team, and the population rallied around the club. After the Civil War, when Union soldiers brought the game home with them, amateur teams flourished, seeking to win for the "glory" of the town.[299] Both Bozeman and Fort Ellis took pride in their teams, as "each boasts of a crack base ball club."[300] The

Thrown Out on Second Base, by Gilbert Gaul, from *Harper's Weekly*, September 10, 1887. A baseball game like those played by Fort Ellis and Bozeman teams.

fort team took special pride in its appearance and used company funds to purchase uniforms and equipment. The uniforms were white with the red letters *F* and *E* across the left breast, white knee breeches, white caps and red stockings.[301]

The importance of the sport to the soldiers frequently outweighed their military duties. In 1868, a player on the team asked to be relieved from guard duty to play a game against the town. The commanding officer emphatically responded:

> *While the game is believed to be healthful and diverting, and one to be encouraged when not incompatible with the interest of service, the inconsiderate presumption manifested the application for the relief of a soldier for such a purpose from one of the most important duties know to the garrison, shows an ignorance of military propriety and a lack of soldierly thought and habit greatly to be deplored.*[302]

The soldiers must have taken his reprimand to heart. In the future, the post team on occasion would leave in the middle of games to attend to their military tasks.[303] In 1878, the military duties of the soldiers forced them to miss the Territorial Championship. The fort's players felt "that the said tournament was not a just criterion of the base ball skill of the Territory." Therefore, the team challenged "the Territory of Montana to a series of games for one hundred dollars a side and the Territorial Championship."[304]

Because of their proximity, and perhaps due to underlying tensions between the soldiers and civilians, a rivalry grew between the fort and town teams. Games could be rough, as the casualty list for one game included a peeled nose, one sprained ankle and "several fingers knocked out of joint."[305] Reported scores between the town and fort teams were often high and lopsided. The soldiers had more free time to practice than did the civilians. Because the military personnel kept roughly the same schedule, practices were also easier to organize. This was evident in 1873, when the fort club beat the town club sixty-four to sixteen. The *Courier* provided an explanation: "This seemingly extraordinary score was made by a club in constant practice and who have been playing together for sometime where as the [town team] had scarcely any practice and the nine that played were not all members of the club."[306]

The town's citizens came to watch the games, and in 1878, the *Courier* reported, "From clapping of hands and waving of handkerchiefs, the game must have been quite interesting." According to the *Helena Herald*, the play of the fort club was indeed good. The newspaper compared the Fort Ellis players to "the finest professionals from the East."[307]

The competition exhibited in the baseball games also spilled over into other activities and further revealed a possible underlying tension. A local man specifically challenged "any soldier of Fort Ellis to a game of Four Ball at $100.00 a side" and was quickly taken up on the offer.[308] However, other competitions indicate no tensions. In 1884, the *Courier* reported that the Bozeman Rod and Gun Club had "a friendly shoot" with the soldiers at the fort, for which "the visiting shooters wish to thank the officers of Fort Ellis for their kind treatment during their visit, every courtesy having been shown them."[309]

As the interactions and friendships between the fort and town grew, the people of Bozeman began to take pride in the "fine body of men" at the fort.[310] The editors of the *Courier* even defended the soldiers of the garrison when the newspapers of other towns attacked them with allegations of drunkenness. Virginia City's newspaper, the *Madisonian*, claimed that "Captain Jackson of Fort Ellis" and a company of troops from the fort "provided with more whisky than clothes" created disturbances in Yellowstone National Park. The *Avant Courier* responded that there was no Captain Jackson at Fort Ellis and no soldiers had been in the park that season. The editor claimed that if such accusations were "a joke it is no less than an insult and if intended as a direct slander without regard, it is a disgrace to the press."[311]

As the economy and society of Bozeman grew and diversified while the numbers of troops at the fort were reduced, some citizens of Bozeman began to resent the presence of the fort. Ranchers' cattle often wandered onto the large military reservation around the post. As early as 1875, the commanding officers took action to isolate the civilian stock and charged the owners for damage to government land.[312] In 1886, the soldiers began driving cattle five to fifteen miles off the reservation, much to the annoyance of the stock's owners. Irate ranchers complained to the editor of the *Courier*, who in turn wrote, "It is hoped the matter complained of may be remedied at once, and our citizens' rights fully respected in this matter."[313]

One of the soldiers who drove off the stock responded through the *Courier*, claiming he was only following orders. He felt that the newspaper was unjustly blaming him and the other enlisted men for these actions. He asked that his letter be published so that everybody may know "the facts of the case, and also to remove some of the prejudice which is unjustly harbored against the soldiers."[314]

A month later, a freighter named Jesse Carter was stopped near the post for not driving on the road. He claimed that he was only trying to avoid a muddy spot that would make travel difficult, but he was briefly detained anyway. Carter reported the incident to the *Courier*, and the editor defended the Civil War veteran's position: "In view of the fact that Mr. Carter faithfully served his country for three years during the late rebellion he does not take kindly to being snubbed in this way…by an officer of the regular army who…has probably never been under fire.[315]

The fact that both the civilians and the soldiers used the newspaper to convey their animosity shows how the newspaper served civic discourse between the two communities. Originally, the *Bozeman Avant Courier* sprang from the ashes of the town's first paper, the *Montana Pick and Plow*, which stopped publication in 1871 after a run of eighteen months. Joseph Wright bought the plant and acted as owner and editor. In 1877, the paper was sold to the merchant, Methodist minister and one-time Blackfoot Indian Agent William W. Alderson. The paper prided itself on the lack of partisan affiliation. That is not to say the paper was without controversy.[316] In 1874, Lester M. Black accused the *Courier* of being under the influence of his rival, Nelson Story. Consequently, Black started his own paper called the *Bozeman Times*, but it was defunct within only ten months. It started up again but eventually was bought out by Alderson and merged with the *Avant Courier*.[317]

Originally, the paper kept abreast of the activities at the fort. The editor even allowed soldiers themselves to write their own column for several years, called "Fort Ellis Items" or "Fort Ellis Jottings," so that the soldiers could share their experiences with the townspeople. Until 1884, the paper published regular items about the fort, but after 1884, it did not record many happenings at Fort Ellis, which may indicate that the importance of the fort to the community had diminished.

The conditions of the frontier helped define the relations between Fort Ellis and Bozeman. Social problems, such as drinking, created both conflict and unity for the two societies. The temperance societies at the fort and in town united in their effort to denounce alcohol and propagate middle-class Protestant values. Even Catholic soldiers embraced these values and organized their own temperance society that maintained their own traditions and ethnic identity. By encouraging such societies, the commanders of the fort and the middle class of the town created stability for their societies as well as agencies that acted to unify their separate communities.

The social relations between the fort and the town were not always equal. The officers tended to associate with the elite middle class of the town. The few single officers who married local women wedded daughters of this set. The enlisted men who joined the temperance society had a greater chance of socializing with "respectable" women than those who did not. The dances and activities of the Templars and other organizations provided an atmosphere that replaced the saloon through other social gatherings with a group that shared a common desire for middle-class status. The soldiers who decided not to engage in temperance activities had more limited opportunities to associate with "respectable" women.

Through military necessity and soldiers' leisure activities, the fort added to the community. The preservation of order and physical improvement of the infrastructure provided the "boosters" of Bozeman with supplementary activities not common to such a small town. The leisure activities in which soldiers participated also provided luxuries that the town might not otherwise have had in its early existence. As Bozeman grew, the fort added to and was an active participant in the development of the town.

CONCLUSION

The reservation is to be thrown open to settlement…it will contribute more to the development of the thrifty little city than its maintenance as a dilapidated two-company post.

By the early 1880s, the town had undergone a vibrant change that brought it out of the adolescent transition stage into that of a secure community. Its population and economy became more diverse, and the physical character of the town gave an air of permanence as the buildings became better constructed and assumed a more regular order. By the time the Northern Pacific Railroad arrived in 1883, Bozeman's existence was not as fragile as it had been when the fort was established sixteen years earlier. A clear sign of the town's security was the new diversity of local commerce. A few establishments offered a variety of products and services in the early years of the settlement, but businesses had become more specialized by the 1880s.[318]

The brick buildings, such as the Tivoli, also indicated a greater confidence in the future, prompting merchants to make a greater investment in the community. William Tracy opened a brick works in the mid-1870s, allowing construction of more permanent buildings. The original log buildings gave way to frame structures, and many of those eventually gave way to brick. Streets became more orderly with a more clearly defined business district separated from residential areas. The town gradually evolved into a more stable and permanent community. It was platted in 1878 and became officially incorporated in 1883. Bozeman organized a fire department in 1884. With

The Tivoli Beer Hall in Bozeman, circa 1880. *Courtesy of Renne Library Special Collections, Montana State University, Bozeman, Montana.*

the growth of stability came a need for more organized schools. Perhaps the greatest indicator of stability and permanence in the young community was the construction of a $14,000 brick school building in 1876–77.

Most of the town had eagerly awaited the coming of the railroad and the access it would provide to eastern markets. The economic importance of the fort began to fade when the trains finally appeared in 1883. The city's future seemed more assured than ever. In addition, the railroad improved the military situation as troops could be moved quickly and with greater ease in the sparsely populated territory. In 1884, the army scaled back the number of troops at the post, removing regiments one at a time, starting with the Second Cavalry, until the fort was only a shadow of its former self. The town gave the troops a warm send-off, recognizing their economic importance in the past but not indicating fear of the economic ramifications of their departure in the future. The mayor, John V. Bogert, addressed the departing cavalry and crowd, proclaiming that the Second Cavalry

> *has followed us and we have followed it. It leaves its dead around us...where its men have fallen in our defense, fighting the enemy...For many years our social and business intercourse have brought them and us into close relation.*[319]

Bogert realized the dynamics of the relationship between the town and the fort. The business relationships brought stability to the area. Despite his warm words, the relationship between the fort and town had become rather sour. The personnel reduction at the fort combined with the railroad's arrival in 1883 and the growing population in the valley caused the settlers to resent the fort's occupation of prime agricultural land. The once-so-important economic input from the fort had lessened, and now townspeople saw the fort as impeding economic development by occupying thirty-two thousand acres of fertile land that could be opened to settlement.[320] Open resentment of the military culminated in the fort's demise.

In 1881, General Sherman lamented that he felt constrained to modify the garrisoning of the West. He stated in his annual report to Congress that many posts were now "absolutely of no use, present or prospective, and should be disposed of." However, he added, "Any attempt to withdraw the garrison or remove the flag is met by local opposition, often impossible to overcome." It therefore must have come as a great pleasure for his successor, General Philip Sheridan, to seize the opportunity and close a post when the citizens of Bozeman petitioned to have the fort closed and the reservation opened to settlement in 1886. Mary Doane, wife of an officer formerly stationed at Fort Ellis, claimed that the petition was started in a moment of "excitement" and that the fort could have continued as an important post for some time, aiding both the military and the territory of Montana. Indeed, her assessment seems correct. In 1882, Sherman had recommended that money be spent to keep Fort Ellis operational for at least ten more years. The citizens of Bozeman were undeterred and pressed their petition, which drew praise from other places in the territory.[321]

Thus, the citizens turned their backs on the post that had helped secure their future. The military presence at Fort Ellis had infused aid at a critical time in the town's early history. The fort had provided a market for Bozeman's main production: agriculture. The soldiers had created an increased demand for retail goods, alcohol and other amenities. By contributing to a stable economy, Fort Ellis relieved the economic crises the town faced and allowed future economic development. The civilians of Bozeman were consciously aware of the economic potential of the fort. They saw it as the duty of the fort to use its financial resources to bolster the local economy. The

Photo of the ceremony when Fort Ellis was being abandoned, 1884. *Courtesy of the Gallatin County Historical Society.*

competition for scarce monetary resources brought friction in addition to economic aid. Many settlers attempted to gain as much government money as possible, even if it meant dishonest actions. Yet by the mid-1880s, the settlers no longer saw a need for the fort. When Fort Ellis closed its gates in 1886, it did not even receive mention in the local newspapers. The editors from a Helena newspaper wrote the final postscript when they joyfully commented that they "can but congratulate the citizens of Bozeman that the reservation is to be thrown open to settlement as it will contribute more to the development of the thrifty little city than its maintenance as a dilapidated two-company post."[322]

In 1867, when the first troops of the Thirteenth United States Infantry came into the Gallatin Valley to build Fort Ellis, Bozeman was a small settlement of fewer than one hundred people with an uncertain future. The people of the small town feared attacks by Indians, had a shrinking market for their abundant agricultural products and were anxious about the future because the dominant male population evinced little interest in putting down roots and creating a stable society. By 1886, when the last troops left Fort Ellis, Bozeman was a thriving community of over one thousand people. The town had created an economically and socially stable community.

Soldiers marching out of Fort Ellis at an unknown date, facing north-northwest. Possibly dates to when the Montana National Guard held an encampment at facility in 1895, almost a decade after the fort was abandoned by the U.S. Army. *Courtesy of the Gallatin County Historical Society.*

The primary mission of Fort Ellis was to defend the fertile Gallatin Valley from incursions of "hostile" natives. The citizens of the valley lived in constant fear of Indian attacks. They exaggerated small incidents and pleaded for help from the garrison at Fort Ellis. When they felt that the fort commanders ignored their appeals for aid, the settlers beseeched higher military or civilian officials for assistance. In the settlers' view, the army should always and without question have been at their disposal for defense against the natives. The settlers and the army rarely agreed on the problems of the Indian frontier. The army was not willing to take hasty actions without higher authority or reasonable cause. The commanders of Fort Ellis had a more sympathetic view of the Indians than the settlers. Even though their duties included protection for the settlers, whom they helped when sufficient danger genuinely arose, the army also had to defend the friendly Indians from the settlers' incursions on the reservations. The limited resources of the post were stretched thin by all the demands of various parties.

Removing the anxiety over the Indian problems denoted only one of the issues facing the new settlement of Bozeman. Though the Gallatin Valley was a tremendously fertile and agriculturally productive area, hard times seemed imminent before the establishment of the fort. Two forces had begun to converge on the region that would likely create economic problems. First, production had outpaced demand in the young territory, and the prices of staples dropped. Second, government officials stopped travel over the Bozeman Trail in the winter of 1867–68. The decrease in the trail's traffic hurt the businesses of Bozeman that stood as the first sentinel of civilization after hundreds of miles of overland travel.

The establishment of Fort Ellis helped curb these forces working against the small town by providing a large market for the crops of the valley. The soldiers' pay helped offset the loss of travelers over the Bozeman Trail by providing a contingent of willing consumers for many commodities and services. The input of Fort Ellis's federal dollars came at a time when it was greatly needed by the citizens of Bozeman.

With relative economic stability, the middle-class citizens and merchant interests of Bozeman sought social stability. Some townsmen went east to find wives since the town afforded few women. By bringing middle-class women to the area, they hoped to bring stability to the town of rowdy men. When the women in the area increased in number, they created a defined middle-class element that changed interactions within the community.

Fort Ellis, on the other hand, was a separate community with a distinct society defined along a rigid caste system between officers and enlisted men. The strong class consciousness and stern formalities spelled out the interaction between soldiers at the fort. Social relations at the fort remained constant as the traditional military system resisted change. The caste system of the fort when it was established in 1867 was the same as when it closed in 1886. Meanwhile, Bozeman had developed from a society of transient males in the late 1860s to an actual community of families with solid social ties by the mid-1880s.

The difference in the societies and the conditions of the frontier defined the relations between the fort and the town. Social problems, particularly excessive drinking, created both conflict and unity between the two societies. Civilians disliked the behavior of drunken soldiers in town, and commanders disliked civilians selling liquor to the soldiers under their command. However, encouraging temperance organizations as a means of combating the problem united the townspeople and soldiers. By encouraging such organizations, the leaders of both communities attempted to create order in their societies.

The attempts to create social stability by advocating middle-class Protestant values in a frontier environment lacking eligible women defined the relationships between the societies. The officers of the post socialized with the town's elite while the enlisted men did not. But those enlisted men who demonstrated their adoption of middle-class values by joining the temperance societies had opportunities to associate with "respectable" women from town. The temperance societies' gatherings acted as a substitute for a saloon and provided a social atmosphere for people who embraced the same vales. The soldiers who did not join temperance societies had a more difficult time associating with "respectable" daughters of the town's families. Consequently, these soldiers associated with the women of more questionable character.

The presence of the fort's authority brought stability through the preservation of order in a location that oftentimes produced violence. In addition, the fort's manpower built and improved the area's infrastructure and provided other amenities that the town of Bozeman might not otherwise have enjoyed at that time in its development. The fort's theater and frequent baseball games provided entertainment not available to other small towns because of their size.

The relationship between the town and the fort was both amicable and antagonistic. However, the fort provided sufficient positive benefits so that the negative aspects of the relationship often were overlooked. By 1886, when the railroad provided another market for the town's goods, when the Indian problem was all but settled and when the population of the town increased to the point that most citizens had little or no personal contact with the soldiers, the relationship began to outgrow the conditions imposed by the frontier.

With the conditions so dramatically changed, Fort Ellis had outlived its usefulness for the civilians of Bozeman. The military reservation occupied a large area of agriculturally viable land that the civilians wanted opened to settlement. The commanders at the fort placed restrictions on the civilians' activities that the settlers did not like. Consequently, the settlers forwarded a petition to the Department of War asking for the closure of the fort and the auctioning off of the reservation. The War Department complied with the petitioners' request, and by August 2, 1886, the last companies had departed from the fort leaving only a small body of men to pack what was left of the government property. The relationship between the fort and the town had come to an end. The *Avant Courier* made its final report on the post that once had been a vital part of the Gallatin Valley. It cryptically stated, "All that Fort Ellis needs to make it a first-class graveyard is a few lying epitaphs."[323] Thus, in just nineteen years (1867–86), Fort Ellis had satisfied the needs of the Gallatin Valley settlers on the western frontier. The fort had provided physical security, expenditures for goods and supplies, soldiers' paychecks

The fort hospital after the post was abandoned. *Courtesy of the Gallatin County Historical Society.*

and social interaction—all of which brought economic, psychological and social stability to the young town and helped shape the fledgling settlement of Bozeman into a stable community.

The buildings of the fort remained in place and were used for a few years by the Montana National Guard but then left to decay. Eventually, they fell into disrepair and were removed as the land was turned over to the Montana Extension Service for use as an experiment station and remains so today. The only indicator of the fort is a granite marker with a bronze plaque placed by the Daughters of the American Revolution in 1976 that briefly commemorates the fort's erection and closure. The plaque, however, gives a much longer commemoration to Captain William Clark of the Lewis and Clark Expedition, who traveled along the East Gallatin River in 1806.

Opposite, bottom: Granite marker at the site of Fort Ellis, placed in 1976 by the Daughters of the American Revolution. The marker stands at what would have been the back of one of the company quarters at the post. The plaque gives only brief mention of the fort but a much longer commemoration to William Clark's passage along the East Gallatin River with a contingent of the Corps of Discovery in 1806. *Author's photo.*

NOTES

Chapter 1

1. Merrill Burlingame, "John M. Bozeman: Montana Trailmaker," *Mississippi Valley Historical Review* 27 (March 1941): 542.
2. Phyllis Smith, *Bozeman and the Gallatin Valley: A History* (Helena, MT: Falcon Press, 1996), 128, 46.
3. M.A. Leeson, *History of Montana, 1739–1885* (New York: Warner, Beers & Co., 1885), 618.
4. Merrill Burlingame, "Unnatural History of Bozeman," Speech to the Q/K Club, Bozeman, Montana, November 18, 1975, Q/K Club File, Special Collections, Renne Library, Montana State University, Bozeman, MT.
5. Ibid.
6. Albert Dickson, *Covered Wagon Days: From the Private Journals of Albert Jerome Dickson* (Lincoln: University of Nebraska Press, 1989), 169.
7. Ibid.
8. Ibid.
9. *Bozeman Avant Courier*, April 14, 1872, 1.
10. Merrill Burlingame, *Montana Frontier* (Helena, MT: State Publishing Co., 1942; Reprint Bozeman, MT: Big Sky Books, 1976), 343.
11. Peter Koch, "Historical Sketch of the Gallatin Valley and Bozeman Pass," in *Contributions to the Historical Society of Montana*, vol. 2 (Helena, MT: State Publishing Company, 1896), 127.

12. Quoted in Robert M. Utley, *Frontier Regulars: The United States Army and the Indian, 1866–1891* (Lincoln: University of Nebraska Press, 1973), 97–8.
13. Ibid., 100.
14. Ibid., 97–8; 105–6.
15. *Senate Executive Documents*, 40th Cong., 1st sess., no. 13 (Washington, D.C.: GPO, 1868), 66.
16. William W. Alderson, Diary, March 23, 1867, Manuscript File 708, Special Collections, Renne Library, Montana State University, Bozeman, MT.
17. Quoted in James Putnam, "Evolution of a Frontier Town: Bozeman, Montana, and Its Search for Economic Stability, 1864–1877" (master's thesis, Montana State University, 1973), 17.
18. Burlingame, *Montana Frontier*, 122–3.
19. It is more likely that John Bozeman's companion Thomas Cover killed Bozeman since his account did not seem to fit the evidence. One theory put forth by Thomas Story, son of Nelson Story, claims that Cover killed Bozeman on behalf of Nelson Story. See Putnam, "Evolution of a Frontier Town," 17.
20. Meagher to Stanton, April 28, 1867, Records of the Office of Secretary of War, Telegrams Received by the Secretary of War, Record Group 107, National Archives; Stanton to Sherman, May 3, 1867, Telegrams Sent by the Secretary of War, Record Group 107, National Archives.
21. Robert G. Athearn, *Thomas Francis Meagher: An Irish Revolutionary in America* (Boulder: University of Colorado Press, 1949), 96; James L. Thane Jr., "The Montana 'Indian War' of 1867," *Arizona and the West* 10, no. 2 (1968), 159.
22. Annual Report of the Secretary of War 1867–1868, 40th Cong. 1st sess., *House Executive Documents* (Washington, D.C.: GPO, 1868), 32; Sherman to Pope, March 9, 1866, Division of the Mississippi, Letters Sent 1865–1866, Records of the War Department, United States Army Command, National Archives; Thane, "Montana 'Indian War,'" 159; Robert Athearn, "General Sherman and the Montana Frontier," *Montana Magazine of History* 3, no. 1 (January 1953), 40.
23. Quoted in Thane, "Montana 'Indian War,'" 161.
24. General W.T. Sherman to Brevet Colonel W.H. Lewis, May 24, 1867, Letter from Secretary of War, 41st Cong. 2nd sess., no. 121, pt. 2 *House Executive Documents* (Washington, D.C.: GPO, 1869); *Montana Post*, July 20, 1867, 3.
25. Report of Brevet Major General Alfred H. Terry, Annual Report of the Secretary of War, 40th Cong., 2nd sess., no. 1, *House Executive Documents* (Washington, D.C.: GPO 1867), 53.

26. Ibid.
27. Koch, "Historical Sketch," 136.
28. Captain R.S. LaMotte to Fort Shaw, August 31, 1867, Records of United States Army Military Commands, Military Posts, Letters Sent, Fort Ellis. Record Group 393, National Archives (hereafter cited as Letters Sent, Fort Ellis).
29. Letter of the Secretary of War, 41st Cong., 3rd sess., *Senate Executive Documents* no. 8 (Washington, D.C.: GPO, 1870), 1–2.
30. Captain R.S. LaMotte to Fort Shaw, August 30, 1867, Letters Sent, Fort Ellis.
31. Governor Green Clay Smith to Adjutant General Department of Dakota, September 13, 1867, Department of Dakota Letters Sent and Received, Record Group 393.
32. Utley, *Frontier Regulars*, 105
33. Ibid., 134.
34. Koch, "Historical Sketch," 136.

CHAPTER 2

35. Major N.B. Sweitzer to Assistant Adjutant General, Department of Dakota, July 31, 1873, Letters Sent, Fort Ellis.
36. Harold L. McElroy, "Mercurial Military: A Study of the Central Montana Frontier Army Policy, *Montana: The Magazine of Western History* 4, no. 4 (1954): 11–2.
37. Sarah J. Bessey Tracey, *The Diary and Reminiscences of Mrs. William H. (Sarah J. Bessey) Tracy*, edited by Merrill Burlingame (Bozeman, MT: Gallatin County Historical Society, 1985), 24. Speech by Mrs. Sarah J. Tracy around the turn of the century.
38. *Bozeman Avant Courier*, September 20, 1871, 3.
39. William "Billy" Frazier, Oral History Interview by Bessie Benham, April 3, 1940, WPA File, Special Collections, Renne Library, Montana State University, Bozeman, MT.
40. *Bozeman Avant Courier*, April 4, 1872, 3.
41. Lester Wilson, quoted in Putnam, "Evolution of a Frontier Town." Published as *Bozeman, Montana*. (Bozeman, MT: Gallatin County Historical Society, 1988), 33.
42. *Bozeman Avant Courier*, May 12, 1872, 3.
43. Ibid., April 4, 1878, 3.

44. Ibid., July 23, 1875, 3.
45. Ibid., April 12, 1877, 3.
46. Governor B.F. Potts to the secretary of the interior, August 2, 1871, National Archives Microfilm, Micro Copy 666, roll 16.
47. Secretary of war to governor of Montana Territory, August 19, 1871, Micro Copy 666, roll 16.
48. Major E.M. Baker to Governor Potts, October 3, 1871, Letters Sent, Fort Ellis.
49. *Bozeman Avant Courier*, February 22, 1872, 3.
50. Ibid., August 22, 1872, 2.
51. Ibid., May 9, 1873, 3.
52. Baker to Potts, October 3, 1873, Letters Sent, Fort Ellis.
53. See Thomas C. Rust, "Settlers, Soldiers, and Scoundrels: Economic Tension in a Frontier Military Town," *Military History of the West* 31, no. 2 (Fall 2001): 117–38.
54. Major N.B. Sweitzer to James Wright, agent for the Crow Indians, April 24, 1874, Letters Sent, Fort Ellis.
55. Utley, *Frontier Regulars*, 51, 52, 55; Michael L. Tate, *The Frontier Army in the Settlement of the West* (Norman: University of Oklahoma Press, 1999), 259.
56. Allan R. Millett and Peter Masloswski, *For the Common Defense: A Military History of the United States of America* (New York: The Free Press, 1994), 253; Utley, *Frontier Regulars*, 45.
57. William B. Skelton, "Army Officers' Attitudes Toward Indians, 1830–1860," *Pacific Northwest Quarterly* 67, no. 3 (1976): 113, 115–6, 124; Tate, *Frontier Army*, 256–9; Utley, *Frontier Regulars*, 54. These sympathetic officers, however, still saw the Indians in terms of white paternalism where the Indian would be best served by adopting "civilization" and Christianity. However, the view of officers was not monolithic, and for every sympathizer, there were also virulent racists. Perhaps most officers felt an ambivalent combination of sympathy, fear and condemnation.
58. "National Indian Policy," 1878, MC 39, Box 3, Brisbin Papers, Montana Historical Society; "Justice to the Indian," 1886, MC39, Box 3, Brisbin Papers.
59. Ibid. Brisbin held a typically patriarchal view of the Indians, however, and he should not be seen as more progressive than he was. He felt Indians should be humanely treated and educated in the ways of Christianity and civilization to help them progress from their more primitive state.
60. "Poetry," SC 1616, James H. Bradley Papers 1864–1879, Montana Historical Society.

61. Ibid.

62. Skelton, "Army Officers' Attitudes," 116.

63. Burlingame, *Montana Frontier*, 115, 117.

64. Robert M. Utley, *The Indian Frontier of the American West, 1846–1890* (Albuquerque: University of New Mexico Press, 1984), 133; Paul A. Hutton, "Phil Sheridan's Pyrrhic Victory: The Piegan Massacre, Army Politics, and the Transfer Debate," *Montana: The Magazine of Western History* 32, no. 2 (1982): 32–43; Robert Wooster, *The Military and United States Indian Policy, 1865–1903* (Lincoln: University of Nebraska Press, 1995), 89.

65. Major N.B. Sweitzer to assistant adjutant general, Department of Dakota, September 9, 1873, Letters Sent, Fort Ellis.

66. Major N.B. Sweitzer to General Phillip Sheridan, commander, Department of Dakota, June 15, 1875, Letters Sent, Fort Ellis.

67. *Bozeman Avant Courier*, March 20, 1877, 3.

68. Captain Edward Ball to commissioner of Indian Affairs, February 18, 1878, James Sanks Brisbin Papers, 1850–1891, MC 39, Box 1, Montana Historical Society; Mark H. Brown, *Plainsmen of the Yellowstone* (New York: G.P. Putnam's Sons, 1961), 438; Michael P. Malone and Richard B. Roeder, "1876 on the Reservations: The Indian 'Question,'" in Paul L. Hedren, ed., *The Great Sioux War 1876–1877* (Helena: Montana Historical Society Press, 1991), 57; Rust, "Settlers, Soldiers, and Scoundrels," 130.

69. D.W. Benham, captain, Seventh Infantry, inspector of Indian suppliers, Crow Agency, Montana, to Major James S. Brisbin, Second U.S. Cavalry, commanding Fort Ellis, February 2, 1877, "Concerning Rations to Crow Agency and Treatment of Indians," James Sanks Brisbin Papers, 1850–1891, MC39, Box 1, Montana Historical Society.

70. Ibid.

71. Wooster, *Military and United States Indian Policy*, 84; Hutton, "Phil Sheridan's Pyrrhic Victory," 33; Raymon L. Welty, "The Indian Policy of the Army 1860–1870," *Cavalry Journal* 36 (1927): 378.

72. Wooster, *Military and United States Indian Policy*, 78; Jill St. Germain, "Feed or Fight: Rationing the Sioux and the Cree, 1868–1885," *Native Studies Review* 16, no. 1 (2005): 73; Utley, *Frontier Regulars*, 59–67.

73. Grant to Stanton, January 15, 1867, Grant Papers, Ser. 5, 47, reel 21, Library of Congress.

74. Wooster, *Military and United States Indian Policy*, 84; Utley, *Indian Frontier*, 96, 213.

75. Hutton, "Phil Sheridan's Pyrrhic Victory," 33–34.
76. Sherman to Sheridan, March 5, 1870, Box 91, Philip H. Sheridan Papers, Manuscript Division, Library of Congress.
77. Sheridan to Sherman, March 18, 1870, Box 91, Philip H. Sheridan Papers, Manuscript Division, Library of Congress.
78. Wooster, *Military and United States Indian Policy*, 210; Utley, *Frontier Regulars*, 59–61, 63, 66.
79. Wooster, *Military and United States Indian Policy*, 39–40.
80. Ibid., 39.
81. Sheridan to Crook, July 16, 1876, Box 58, Philip H. Sheridan Papers, Manuscript Division, Library of Congress.
82. Wooster, *Military and United States Indian Policy*, 211; Leo E. Olivia, "The Army and the Indian," *Military Affairs* 38, no. 3 (October 1974): 117; Alvin M. Josephy Jr., "Indian Policy and the Battle of the Little Bighorn," in Charles E. Rankin, ed., *Legacy: New Perspectives on the Battle of the Little Bighorn* (Helena: Montana Historical Society, 1996), 23, 38.
83. Sherman to Schofield, June 9, 1869, Records of the Adjutant General's Office, Letters Sent, Fort Ellis, Record Group 94, National Archives.
84. *Bozeman Avant Courier*, March 21, 1872, 3.
85. Ibid., January 23, 1874, 3.
86. James S. Hutchins, "Poison in the Pemmican: The Yellowstone Wagon-Road and Prospecting Expedition of 1874," *Montana: The Magazine of Western History* 8, no. 3 (1958): 10.
87. *Bozeman Avant Courier*, January 9, 1874, 3; January 16, 1874, 3.
88. Major N.B. Sweitzer to assistant adjutant general, Department of Dakota, January 22, 1874, Letters Sent, Fort Ellis.
89. Headquarters, Department of Dakota, to Commanding Officer, Fort Ellis, August 2, 1873, Records of Divisions, Department of Dakota, Letters Sent, Fort Ellis, Record Group 393, National Archives.
90. *Bozeman Avant Courier*, March 27, 1874, 2.
91. Ibid., February 27, 1874, 2.
92. Leeson, *History of Montana*, 619.
93. Major Sweitzer to adjutant general, Department of Dakota, May 1, 1874, Letters Sent, Fort Ellis; Major Sweitzer to Governor B.F. Potts, May 2, 1874, Letters Sent, Fort Ellis.
94. Secretary of the interior to Governor B.F. Potts, March 10, 1874, Records of the Office of the Secretary of the Department of Interior, Telegrams Sent, Record Group 48, National Archives.

95. B.F. Potts to secretary of the interior, March 12, 1874, Records of the Office of the Secretary of the Department of Interior, Telegrams Received, Record Group 48, National Archives.
96. *Bozeman Avant Courier*, May 22, 1874, 3.
97. Ibid., January 29, 1875, 3.
98. Ibid., April 9, 1875, 3.
99. Captain D.W. Benham to acting assistant adjutant general, Distract of Montana, June 15, 1875, Letters Sent, Fort Ellis.
100. Major James S. Brisbin to assistant adjutant general, Department of Dakota, February 19, 1876, Letters Sent, Fort Ellis.
101. Major James S. Brisbin to Brevet Major General Gibbon, February 20, 1876, Letters Sent, Fort Ellis.
102. Wooster, *Military and United States Indian Policy*, 164.
103. Edgar I. Stewart, "Major Brisbin's Relief of Fort Pease," in Paul Hedren, ed., *The Great Sioux War, 1876–1877* (Helena: Montana Historical Society Press, 1991), 118–21.
104. Robert M. Utley, "A Chained Dog: The Indian-Fighting Army. Military Strategy on the Western Frontier," *American West* 10, no. 4 (1973): 18.
105. *Bozeman Avant Courier*, July 7, 1876, 3.
106. Burlingame, *Montana Frontier*, 241.
107. Wooster, *Military and United States Indian Policy*, 212–3.

CHAPTER 3

108. Daniel S. Tuttle, "Early History of the Episcopal Church in Montana," Contributions to the Montana Historical Society 5 (1904): 314.
109. Special Order No. 39, December 11, 1867, Fort Ellis, Montana, Special Order Book, Records of the U.S. Continental Commands, 1821–1920, Record Group 393, National Archives, Washington, D.C. (hereafter cited as Fort Ellis, Special Order Book).
110. Special Order No. 41, December 14, 1867, Fort Ellis, Special Order Book.
111. Special Order No. 42, December 15, 1867, Fort Ellis, Special Order Book.
112. *Bozeman Avant Courier*, March 28, 1873, 3.
113. Ibid., November 7, 1874, 3.
114. Burlingame, *Montana Frontier*, 211.
115. U.S. Senate. "Report of Lt. Colonel Samuel B. Holabird of a Reconnaissance made by Him in the Department of Dakota in 1869,"

Senate Executive Documents, 41st Cong., 3rd sess., no. 3 (Washington, D.C.: GPO, 1871), 31.

116. Captain D.P. Hancock to Major O.D. Greene, acting adjutant general, Department of Dakota, August 11, 1872, Letters Sent, Fort Ellis.
117. Ibid.
118. Don Rickey Jr., *Forty Miles a Day on Beans and Hay: The Enlisted Soldier Fighting the Indian Wars* (Norman: University of Oklahoma Press, 1963), 111.
119. Frances M. Roe, *Army Letters from an Officer's Wife, 1871–1888* (New York: Appleton, 1909; Reprint Lincoln: University of Nebraska Press, 1981), 124, 166.
120. Burlingame, *Montana Frontier*, 204.
121. Ibid., 340.
122. Lieutenant Colonel C.G. Gilbert, Fort Shaw, to D. Hanahan, United States Indian agent to the Flathead Indians, October 14, 1875, Letters Sent, Fort Shaw, Montana Territory.
123. Rickey, *Forty Miles*, 97.
124. Burlingame, *Montana Frontier*, 340.
125. Ibid., 343.
126. Ibid.
127. *Montana Pick and Plow*, March 10, 1870, 1.
128. Ibid.
129. *Bozeman Avant Courier*, March 14, 1872, 3; March 28, 1872, 3.
130. Ibid., March 15, 1879, 3.
131. Ibid., October 26, 1871, 3.
132. William "Billy" Frazier, interview by Bessie Benham April 3, 1940. WPA File, Special Collections, Renne Library, Montana State University, Bozeman, MT.
133. *Bozeman Avant Courier*, July 4, 1873, 3.
134. Ibid., July 11, 1873, 3.
135. Special Order No. 62, May 13, 1876, Fort Ellis, Special Order Book.
136. U.S. War Department, "United States Army, Adjutant General's Office Returns, Fort Ellis, Montana Territory," Microcopy 617, Film 396, Rolls 347 and 348.
137. Circular No. 27, April 4, 1877, Records of United States Army Military Commands, Military Posts, Circular Book, Fort Ellis, Record Group 393, National Archives.
138. Utley, *Frontier Regulars*, 59-63.
139. *Bozeman Avant Courier*, May 16, 1877, 3.
140. Ibid., May 23, 1877, 3.

141. Ibid., December 21, 1871, 2.
142. Ibid.
143. Ibid., December 28, 1871, 3; January 11, 1872, 2; Frazier, interview.
144. U.S. Senate. "Report of Lt. Colonel Samuel B. Holabird of a Reconnaissance Made by Him in the Department of Dakota in 1869," *Senate Executive Documents*, 41st Cong., 3rd sess., no. 3 (Washington, D.C.: GPO, 1871), 2.
145. Ibid., 2–3.
146. Interview with Malcolm Story, quoted in Putnam, "Evolution of a Frontier Town," 30.
147. Frazier, interview.
148. Captain Edward Ball to commissioner of Indian Affairs, February 18, 1878, Manuscript Collection 39, Box 1, Folder 20, Montana Historical Society, Helena, MT.
149. Ibid.; Brown, *Plainsmen of the Yellowstone*, 438.
150. William White, Diary, January 26 and February 13, 1876, Manuscript File 515, Special Collections, Montana State University, Bozeman, MT.
151. Ibid., February 13, 1876.
152. General Order No. 55, December 7, 1876, Records of United States Army Military Commands, Military Posts, Fort Ellis, Montana Territory, General Order Book, Record Group 393, National Archives.
153. Ibid.
154. White, Diary, February 8, 1876.
155. Edward M. Coffman, *The Old Army: A Portrait of the American Army in Peacetime, 1874–1898* (New York: Oxford University Press, 1986), 21–2.
156. White, Diary, January 28, 1876.
157. General Order No. 1, January 13, 1873; General Order No. 10, March 21, 1873; General Order No. 16, April 10, 1873, Fort Ellis, General Order Book.
158. General Order, No. 5, February 22, 1872, Fort Ellis, General Order Book. These are only the ones who left without permission. Also see General Order No. 18, February 12, 1876; Special Order No. 39, December 11, 1867, and Special Order No. 41, December 14, 1867, Fort Ellis, Special Order Book.
159. General Order No. 70, November 16, 1875, Fort Ellis, General Order Book; *Bozeman Avant Courier*, October 11, 1871, 3.
160. General Order No. 15, 11 November 1869, Fort Ellis, General Order Book; General Order No. 4, January 13, 1873; and General Order No. 31, December 10, 1870.

161. *Bozeman Avant Courier*, March 20, 1879, 3.
162. Ibid., May 10, 1877, 3.
163. Ibid., February 12, 1880, 3.
164. Tenth Census of the United States, 1880, Population Schedule, Records of the Bureau of the Census (Microfilm T9, reel 742); Smith, *Bozeman and the Gallatin Valley*, 128.
165. "Receipts for Materials from Quartermasters Stores, Fort Ellis, 1884," Manuscript File 851, Special Collections, Renne Library, Montana State University, Bozeman, MT.
166. *Bozeman Avant Courier*, May 15, 1874, 3.
167. Ibid., July 19, 1877, 3.
168. Special Order No. 59, June 4, 1869, Fort Ellis, Special Order Book.
169. Leeson, *History of Montana*, 593.
170. Ibid., 340.
171. *Bozeman Avant Courier*, June 12, 1884, 3.

CHAPTER 4

172. U.S. War Department, "United States Army, Adjutant General's Post Returns," Fort Ellis, Montana, June 1870, National Archives Microfilm 396, Micro Copy 617, Roll 347.
173. On each schedule, there were some individuals who did not list a place of birth. All percentages for place of birth are computed based on those who listed a place of birth.
174. Oliver Knight, *Life and Manners of the Frontier Army* (Norman: University of Oklahoma Press; 1978), 72–3, 79.
175. West Point Alumni Foundation, *Registrar of Graduates and Former Cadets of the United States Military Academy, 1802–1965* (West Point, NY: West Point Alumni Foundation, 1965).
176. Montana Institute of the Arts, Bozeman Branch, History Group, "Historical Map of Gallatin County," 1951, Special Collections, Renne Library, Montana State University, Bozeman, MT.
177. Roe, *Army Letters*, ix–x.
178. West Point Alumni Foundation.
179. James L. Morrison Jr., "Circumstances of Parents of Cadets, 1842–1879," Appendix One in *The Best School in the World: West Point, The Pre-Civil War Years, 1833–1866* (Kent, OH: Kent State University Press, 1986), 155–7.

180. Stephen E. Ambrose, *Duty, Honor and Country: A History of West Point* (Baltimore, MD: Johns Hopkins Press, 1966), 127; Coffman, *Old Army*, 252; Knight, *Life and Manners*, 72.
181. Ambrose, *Duty, Honor and Country*, 147.
182. Ibid.; Morrison, "Circumstances," 92.
183. Ambrose, *Duty, Honor and Country*, 191.
184. George S. Pappas, *To the Point: The United States Military Academy, 1802–1902* (West Port, CT: Praeger, 1993), 363–79.
185. Rickey, *Forty Miles*, 64.
186. Ibid., 66.
187. General Order No. 18, April 16, 1869, Fort Ellis, General Order Book.
188. *Bozeman Avant Courier*, April 3, 1874, 3.
189. Ibid., February 12, 1880, 3.
190. Ibid., March 11, 1880, 3.
191. Leeson, *History of Montana*, 622.
192. *Bozeman Avant Courier*, February 12, 1880, 3.
193. U.S. War Department, *A Report on the Hygiene of the United States Army with Descriptions of Military Posts, Circular No. 8* (Washington, D.C.: GPO, 1875), 406.
194. White, Diary, February 12, 13 and 14, 1876.
195. Knight, *Life and Manners*, 42.
196. Plans of Fort Ellis, 1868, 1876, 1878, 1884, Montana Map File, Special Collections, Renne Library, Montana State University, Bozeman, MT.
197. Knight, *Life and Manners*, 43; Coffman, *Old Army*, 294–5.
198. Coffman, *Old Army*, 294, 296; Knight, *Life and Manners*, 42.
199. Daniel W. Howe, "Victorian Culture in America," in *Victorian America*, edited by Daniel Walker Howe (Philadelphia: University of Pennsylvania Press, 1976), 22–3.
200. *Bozeman Avant Courier*, January 1, 1880, 3.
201. Knight, *Life and Manners*, 42–4, 120.
202. Albert G. Brackett, "Our Cavalry: Its Duties, Hardships, and Necessities at Our Frontier Posts," *Journal of Military Service Institutes* 4 (1892): 387.
203. Roe, *Army Letters*, ix.
204. Ibid., 230.
205. Ibid., 316, 230.
206. U.S. War Department, *Hygiene of the United States Army*, 407.
207. Ibid., 405.
208. Richard White, *It's Your Misfortune and None of My Own: A New History of the American West* (Norman: University of Oklahoma Press, 1991), 298–9, 302.

209. Ibid.
210. Quoted in Esther C. Niebel, *A Century of Service: The First Methodist Church, Bozeman, Montana* (Bozeman, MT: First Methodist Church, 1966), 3.
211. Tracy, *Diary and Reminiscences*, 19.
212. Ibid., 32–4.
213. Ibid., 29, editor's note by Merrill Burlingame, 36.
214. White, *It's Your Misfortune*, 304.
215. Merrill Burlingame, *Law and Order in Gallatin County: Jails, Courthouses, Detention Centers, and Terminal Justice* (Bozeman, MT: Gallatin County Historical Society, 1987), 5. According to the 1880 census, other prostitutes with different regional identities were employed, including some from the United States and Europe.
216. Mrs. William J. Beall, "Bozeman's First Schools," in *Contributions to the Montana Historical Society*, Vol. 2 (Helena: Montana Historical Society, 1896), 304.
217. Beall, "Bozeman's First Schools," 304–411. Many young women came to the West to teach because of demographic changes in the East. Declining numbers of men postponed marriage, giving women no guarantee of marriage upon reaching adulthood. Also see White, *It's Your Misfortune*, 313.
218. White, *It's Your Misfortune*, 313; Beall, "Bozeman's First Schools," 304.
219. Beall, "Bozeman's First Schools," 304–11.
220. Ibid., 310.
221. White, *It's Your Misfortune*, 311; Lina M. Houston, *Early History of Gallatin County, Montana* (Bozeman, MT: Bozeman Daily Chronicle, 1933), 26.
222. Niebel, *Century of Service*, 19; Leeson, *History of Montana*, 621.
223. White, *It's Your Misfortune*, 311.
224. Houston, *Early History*, 27–8; Daniel S. Tuttle, "Early History of the Episcopal Church in Montana," in *Contributions to the Historical Society of Montana*, Vol. 5 (Helena, MT: State Publishing Society, 1904), 314.
225. Leeson, *History of Montana*, 629.
226. Ibid., 628.
227. Ibid., 629–30; White, *It's Your Misfortune*, 318.
228. Michael P. Malone and Richard B. Roeder, *Montana: A History of Two Centuries* (Seattle: University of Washington Press, 1976), 75; Burlingame, *Montana Frontier*, 155.
229. Ellis L. Waldron, *Montana Politics Since 1864* (Missoula: University of Montana Press, 1958), 24; *Bozeman Avant Courier*, December 1, 1881, 3.

230. Matt W. Alderson, *Bozeman: A Guide to Its Places of Recreation and a Synopsis of Its Superior National Advantages, Industries, and Opportunities* (Bozeman, MT: Bozeman Avant Courier, 1883), 34.

CHAPTER 5

231. *Bozeman Avant Courier*, February 7, 1873, 3; see also Burlingame, *Law and Order*, 3–7.
232. John J. Rumburger, *Power, Profits, and Prohibition: Alcohol Reform and the Industrializing of America 1800–1930* (Albany: State University of New York Press, 1898), 7; Ian R. Tyrrell, *Sobering Up: From Temperance to Prohibition in Antebellum America, 1800–1860* (Westport, CT: Greenwood Press, 1979), 319–20.
233. Tyrrell, *Sobering Up*, 317–8, 321.
234. W.J. Rorabaugh, *The Alcoholic Republic: An American Tradition* (New York: Oxford University Press, 1979), 144; Rickey, *Forty Miles*, 158.
235. Joseph R. Gusfield, *Symbolic Crusade: Status, Politics, and the American Temperance Movement* (Chicago: University of Illinois Press, 1963), 4–5.
236. Quote from manuscript in "Fort Custer-Fort Sarpy, Place" File, unpublished, untitled, author unknown, written for submission to *Harper's Magazine*, late 1870s, Microfiche 83, Montana Vertical File, Special Collections, Renne Library, Montana State University, Bozeman, MT.
237. Rickey, *Forty Miles*, 20; Gusfield, *Symbolic Crusade*, 4–5; Rorabaugh, *Alcoholic Republic*, 238–9.
238. Rorabaugh, *Alcoholic Republic*, 248.
239. General Order No. 5, February 22, 1872, Fort Ellis, General Order Book. It must be kept in mind that these are the only ones who left without permission.
240. General Order No. 41, October 16, 1872, Fort Ellis, General Order Book.
241. General Order No. 47, August 14, 1873, Fort Ellis, General Order Book.
242. General Order No. 18, February 12, 1876, Fort Ellis, General Order Book.
243. General Order No. 70, November 16, 1875, Fort Ellis, General Order Book.
244. Knight, *Life and Manners*, 226.
245. Tuttle, "Early History," 314. Bishop Tuttle claimed that even though Captain LaMotte was uncompromising in his attitude toward alcohol, some of the other officers were not. He felt that some of LaMotte's junior officers "were not altogether comfortable" under his position, 211; Special Order No. 39, December 11, 1867, Fort Ellis, Special Order Book; Special Order No. 41, December 14, 1867, Fort Ellis, Special Order Book.

246. Ernest H. Cherrington, *The Evolution of Prohibition in the United States of America: A Chronological History of the Liquor Problem and the Temperance Reform in the United States from the Earliest Settlements to the Consummation of National Prohibition* (Westerville, OH: American Issue Press, 1920), 145, 161–2.
247. Ibid.; White, *It's Your Misfortune*, 361.
248. White, *It's Your Misfortune*, 361.
249. Leeson, *History of Montana*, 622.
250. White, Diary, January 20, 1876.
251. *Bozeman Avant Courier*, "Fort Ellis Jottings," February 12, 1880, 3.
252. By the turn of the century, 74 percent of all regular communicants in Montana were Catholic, twice the national average. This may have been due to the large immigrant Irish population in Butte during the 1880s, but the Catholics had a long presence in the territory and state. See Malone and Roeder, *Montana*, 269.
253. Burlingame, *Montana Frontier*, 300.
254. Ibid.; Malone and Roeder, *Montana*, 269.
255. Circular No. 13, March 28, 1878, Records of United States Army Military Commands, Military Posts, Circular Book, Fort Ellis, Record Group 393, National Archives.
256. Gusfield, *Symbolic Crusade*, 4–5, 16.
257. G. Towey and M.L. Sullivan, "The Knights of Father Mathew: Parallel Ethnic Reform," *Missouri Historical Review* 75 (January 1981): 168, 175.
258. *Bozeman Avant Courier*, February 12, 1880, 3.
259. Ibid., February 5, 1880, 3.
260. Ibid., February 27, 1880, 3.
261. Ibid., June 16, 1874, 3.
262. White, *It's Your Misfortune*, 361; Rickey, *Forty Miles*, 161–2.
263. *Bozeman Avant Courier*, August 14, 1874, 3; February 22, 1873, 3.
264. Ibid., June 11–July 5, 1877, 3.
265. Ibid., April 4, 1873, 3.
266. Ibid., June 24, 1880, 3.
267. Roe, *Army Letters*, 233–4.
268. *Bozeman Avant Courier*, June 24, 1880, 3.
269. Ibid., September 26, 1878, 3.
270. Ibid., July 29, 1885, 3.
271. Ibid., July 5, 1877, 3.
272. Patricia Stallard, *Glittering Misery: Dependent of the Indian Fighting Army* (Norman: University of Oklahoma Press, 1978), 47.
273. *Bozeman Avant Courier*, October 24, 1873, 3; October 31, 1873, 3.

274. Merrill Burlingame, "Beginnings in Bozeman," quoted in Putnam, 26.
275. *Bozeman Avant Courier*, January 3, 1878, 3.
276. Roe, *Army Letters*, 331.
277. Ibid.
278. *Bozeman Avant Courier*, February 5, 1880, 3.
279. White, Diary, January 4, 1876.
280. *Bozeman Avant Courier*, December 16, 1880, 3.
281. "Fort Custer-Fort Sarpy, Places."
282. U.S. War Department, *Hygiene of the United States Army*, 51.
283. "Fort Custer-Fort Sarpy, Places"; U.S. War Department, *Hygiene of the United States Army*, 407–8; White, *It's Your Misfortune*, 305.
284. Anne M. Butler, *Daughters of Joy, Sisters of Mercy: Prostitutes in the American West, 1865–1890* (Urbana: University of Illinois Press, 1985), 68; "Vital Statistics of Bozeman from Its Newspapers," Film 586, Special Collections, Renne Library, Montana State University, Bozeman, MT; *Bozeman Avant Courier*, January 16, 1874, 3; November 22, 1883, 3.
285. *Bozeman Avant Courier*, August 14, 1874, 3; Orrin Bonney and Loraine Bonney, *Battle Drums and Geysers: The Life and Remarkable Career of Lieutenant G.C. Doane* (New York: Knopf and Company, 1970), 96.
286. Bonney and Bonney, *Battle Drums*, 96.
287. Merrill Burlingame, "The Influence of the Military in the Building of Montana," *Pacific Northwest Quarterly* 7 (Autumn 1938): 135–49.
288. *Bozeman Avant Courier*, February 18, 1877, 3.
289. Ibid., February 5, 1880, 3; February 12, 1880, 3.
290. Burlingame, *Montana Frontier*, 329–30. Fort Shaw also had a comic troupe named the "Fort Shaw Comedy Company." However, there was not an established civilian settlement nearby, and the productions were mainly for the soldiers of the garrison. Fort Keogh formed a theatrical company following the development of the town of Miles City when the fort was established.
291. "Fort Custer-Fort Sarpy, Places."
292. *Bozeman Avant Courier*, March 21, 1873, 3.
293. Ibid., February 6, 1877, 3.
294. Ibid., December 8, 1874, 3; see also similar sentiments on February 6, 1874, and November 13, 1879.
295. Ibid., November 21, 1873, 3.
296. Ibid., February 8, 1872, 3.
297. Ibid., June 6, 1872, 3.

298. John Helyar, *Lords of the Realm: The Real History of Baseball* (New York: Villard Books, 1994), 3.
299. David Voigt, *American Baseball*, Vol. 1 (University Park: Pennsylvania State University Press, 1983), 12.
300. *Bozeman Avant Courier*, "Base Ball," May 9, 1873, 3.
301. Ibid., "Local News," June 27, 1873, 3.
302. General Order No. 28, September 27, 1868, Fort Ellis, General Order Book.
303. *Bozeman Avant Courier*, May 20, 1880, 3.
304. Ibid., April 17, 1879, 3.
305. Ibid., "Base Ball," 3.
306. Ibid., June 27, 1873, 3.
307. Ibid., April 11, 1878, 3; October 10, 1873, 3.
308. Ibid., January 8, 1877, 3; January 15, 1877, 3.
309. Ibid., June 26, 1884, 3.
310. Ibid., May 23, 1872, 3
311. Ibid., September 18, 1874, 3.
312. General Order No. 31, June 23, 1875, Fort Ellis, General Order Book.
313. *Bozeman Avant Courier*, June 10, 1886, 3.
314. Ibid., June 17, 1880, 3.
315. Ibid., July 15, 1886, 3.
316. Houston, *Early History*, 34–5.
317. Putnam, "Evolution of a Frontier Town," 24.

CONCLUSION

318. Tenth Census of the United States; Smith, *Bozeman and the Gallatin Valley*, 128.
319. *Bozeman Avant Courier*, June 12, 1884, 3.
320. Mary Hunter Doane, "History of Fort Ellis," Manuscript Collection 2211, Box 2, Folder 12, Special Collections, Renne Library, Montana State University, Bozeman, MT.
321. Report of the Secretary of War, *House Executive Documents*, 47th Cong., 1st sess., no. 1, pt. 2, vol. 2 (Washington, D.C.: GPO, 1882), 35. Fort Ellis was not at that time one of the posts he was considering closing. See Report of the Secretary of War, *House Executive Documents*, 47th Cong., 2nd sess., no. 1, pt. 2, vol. 2 (Washington, D.C.: GPO, 1882), 12–13, 15; Mary Hunter Doane, "History of Montana Forts," undated Manuscript

File 2045, Special Collections, Renne Library, Montana State University; *Helena Independent*, August, 4, 1886, 2.

322. *Helena Independent*, August 4, 1886, 2.
323. *Bozeman Avant Courier*, November 25, 1886, 3.

INDEX

A

B

C

D

E

F

Y

ABOUT THE AUTHOR

Dr. Tom Rust is an associate professor of history and a native of Bozeman, Montana, who graduated from the University of Minnesota with a BA in history in 1992. He received his MA in history in 1995 from the University in Denver, where his work in American military history, more specifically the nineteenth-century West, has been published in the journal *Military History of West*. He completed his PhD at the University of Leicester in 2006. He has conducted and published both historical and archaeological research in a variety of areas from ancient Rome to the American West. Dr. Rust has taught at Montana State University–Billings since 1999.

Visit us at
www.historypress.net

This title is also available as an e-book